The Advantage of Being Born Poor

by Ernie Buresh

with Dave Rasdal

DEDICATION

This book is dedicated to my loving wife, Joanne, and to our daughters, Wendy and Sandy.

CONTENTS

A Poor Childhood

A Working Guy

A Future to Bank On

Friends, Family and Fun

Retirement isn't an Option

A Poor Childhood

ERNIE BURESH

Chapter 1

Cardboard Shoes,

Odd Overalls

and Corduroy Pants

About the time the United States fell into The Great Depression, I started school. We were poor already, so I'm not sure the bad economy really affected us. I was only five, so it never really mattered to me. It was the only life I'd known.

What mattered was that my brother, Les, more than four years older than me, had been going to school since I could remember.

We had just moved to rural Iowa after having lived in Western, a small community a few miles south of today's Kirkwood Community College campus in southwest Cedar Rapids. Western wasn't much of a town then and isn't any bigger today. At one time it had a college, but that was way before our time there even though one of the big old buildings – I think it was the main one with classrooms – still stood in town.

3

My mother, Emma, in her early 30s, and my father, Joe, a couple of years younger, had grown up on hilly, less-than-prosperous farms south of Western near Shueyville. I guess they thought opportunities were better in town.

An envelope more than 80 years old includes the return address for Western Garage operated by Joe Buresh.

In Western, my father worked in our garage repairing cars. I suppose he had a "shingle" out front advertising that fact, but I don't remember it. I think he worked on the same cars over and over because that's how reliable they were in the 1920s. I liked to watch him work on cars during the day, but stayed away from him at night when he drank his beer and became a different man.

When she wasn't taking care of me, my mother cleaned houses in the area for a couple of dollars, raised chickens and baked a lot. She often packed up her kolaches to sell at The Roundhouse in the Czech Village in Cedar Rapids. We were Czech, but we were

4

different than most of the rest. We weren't Catholic and we rarely went to church.

My mother also spent a lot of time at her huge rug loom – it was bigger than I was. I'd watch her weave the shuttle in and out of the other threads that she kept tight in the loom with her foot pedal. She'd buy old clothes at garage sales, tear them up into long strips, tie them together and then weave her rag rugs. She would sell them at The Roundhouse, too. She didn't know it was called recycling. It was simply a way to earn extra money.

My mother kept an eye on the household budget. At garage sales she'd also buy us clothes to wear. We didn't go shopping in real stores much except for Christmas and then it was mostly window shopping. We saw the wish books, too, from Sears and Montgomery Ward, but they soon ended up as toilet paper in the outhouse.

I don't remember much about moving to the farm east of Western, but my father must have grown tired of rapping his knuckles against car frames when he turned wrenches. He thought he could make a go of farming again, but the place he rented wasn't much better than what he'd grown up on, from what I later understood.

So, when I started kindergarten, I walked to the nearby Buresh one-room school. At the time, I didn't really think about my last name being the same, and it's probably a good thing. There was a Buresh Cemetery there, too, and it might have given me nightmares to think about dead people and ghosts.

What I do remember are my second-hand shoes, my overalls without the brass buttons and my first brand new pair of pants – corduroys that whistled when I walked.

Kids have always been hard on shoes. You run, you jump, you slip and slide. You drag them in the dirt, scuff them up taking a shortcut through weeds and grow out of them faster than a baby chicken hatches from an egg.

When you don't have any money to buy new shoes, you make do. That's when my mother would get out the cardboard and scissors. It was flat cardboard and easy to cut. She'd put my shoe on it as a template and cut around it, then stuff the cardboard in the bottom of the shoe. That way, she covered up the hole in the sole and also insulated the edges where the stitching of the upper part of the shoe had begun to work loose.

New shoes, they weren't. But it worked, for a couple of years, anyway. So, farming must have been OK, because I don't remember ever again having to worry about friends seeing the cardboard whenever I'd remove my shoes in public.

Ernie Buresh (second from the left) poses with students from his rural Shueyville elementary school. Note Ernie's overalls.

My clothes were another story, altogether. I look at school class pictures of me before I was ten and there I am in the front row wearing overalls of a different stripe. The stripes seem further apart and more pronounced. I don't have all the pockets the other boys have. And my overalls don't have the brass buttons on either side of the waist that hold them together.

Nobody ever called me names because I wore different clothes. My overalls never led to any fights or to ostracism from group activities, either. But I knew, inside, that not being like the other boys made it difficult for them to become my friends.

Then, maybe a couple of years later, my mother bought me my first pair of new pants. The dark brown corduroys were the slickest things I'd ever worn. I felt taller. I thought I could run faster and that other kids would want to be my friend because I had new pants.

By then I was in the band. I played the trombone which was a disaster. I wasn't musically inclined. I wasn't really good at anything. It was an excuse to hang around with the other kids.

One night we'd finished band practice and it was dark. For years, we'd race to the edge of the school property. It was what kids did. We loved to have foot races. But this night, in the fall, somebody suggested we steal some watermelons from a neighbor's garden. I went along with the crowd. We picked up some watermelons and then something spooked us. A noise or a light. We ran as fast as we could. I didn't see the fence.

I don't recall how bad the tear was in my new corduroys, only that they got tangled up in the fence and I feared they'd been shredded like the cloth my mother used on her rug loom. The walk home was both long and short, if you know what I mean, because I dawdled as best I could knowing that I'd get a bawling out.

What I do remember is that my father wasn't there. My mother wouldn't hit me. She was angry, I'm sure, but she doled out punishment in her own gentle way.

And she sewed up my brand new corduroys and sent me off to school the same way she did when I had cardboard in my shoes and the overalls without the brass trim.

You can only be young once. You won't always have your mother to send you off to school in the best way she knows how, with her encouragement and her love.

The women of Ernie's family are, front row, left to right, Emma Stanek Buresh (his mother), Elma Hrdlicka Buresh (his uncle's wife) and Doris Krob Buresh (his brother's wife). Back row, from left, Georgia Buresh (his father's sister), Mary Buresh (his father's mother) and Barbara Stanek (his mother's mother).

Chapter 2

Observations:

Ernie Goes Home

Fallen leaves skitter across the still green grass in front of the gate to the tiny Buresh Cemetery a couple of miles east of Western, Iowa. Only a handful of pure white clouds drift across an otherwise pale autumn sky. And, gazing out the driver's side window of his Chrysler minivan, Ernie Buresh gently strokes the gray and white curly fur of Mattie, the 14-year-old toy Shih Tzu that he and his wife, Joanne, adopted after the death of their daughter, Sandy.

Ernie, who celebrated his 88th birthday just three days earlier, didn't know anyone who has been buried in Buresh Cemetery. Ernie's parents were laid to rest in the Czech National Cemetery in Cedar Rapids. Sandy was interred in a mausoleum at Cedar Memorial in Cedar Rapids.

But Buresh Cemetery – its words outlined in an intricate sign above the open gate that leads to tombstones as old as the Civil War – reminds Ernie of two things. First, the name Buresh is as popular in his ancestors' homeland, today's Czech Republic, as Smith is in the United States. And, second, as a child more than 80 years ago, this is the area where Ernie lived.

Buresh Cemetery is a couple of miles east of Western.

Ernie would walk along this gravel road and many others to attend school and to play, to visit friends and relatives, to grow up and learn dozens of indelible lessons that would serve him well as an adult.

"I wish I would have kept a diary," Ernie says. "That would have helped. I wish I would have put the dates on all my pictures. That would have really helped."

For 20 years, and maybe longer – through a life that included 52 years in the banking industry, a marriage that's still going strong after 65 years and raising Sandy, a daughter who needed special attention – Ernie's friends have told him he should write a book.

In 2004, Ernie alluded to the fact he had taken his friends' advice to heart. In an article published that year in the Iowa State University Alumni newsletter, he advised students to be financially responsible and to avoid over extending themselves with credit, adding that those philosophies were included in a book he was writing that was to be titled, "The Advantage of Being Born Poor."

So, Ernie had the idea and the title. But he didn't seem to have the time until now.

"I don't want it to be about me," Ernie says about this book. "I'm nobody. I'm just a guy who grew up poor and learned from that."

Contrary to Ernie's opinion, his life shows that someone with the right attitude can become successful. You just need to pay attention. You need to learn from your mistakes. You need to listen to advice from others but have confidence in yourself to make the right decisions. You need to make friends and keep them close. You need to grab each opportunity when it presents itself. You need to . . .

"Life is a succession of lessons which must be lived to be understood," said Helen Keller, who famously overcame her deafness and blindness to earn an education, to write and lecture, to serve as a model for everyone who had odds to overcome.

Any journey of reflection must start somewhere. Since Ernie has enlisted my help in putting together his book, I have suggested we begin by going home.

Ernie puts his minivan in drive and guides it along the hilly gravel roads and twisting blacktops of Linn and Johnson counties, of Western and Shueyville, of Swisher and back to Cedar Rapids.

A grove of leafless trees is all that stands where the whitewashed one-room Buresh School once welcomed Ernie to his first year of formal lessons. Ranch homes have replaced old two-story farmhouses and metal pole buildings have been erected where old barns once served as the center of the farm. In the rural areas, one brick farmhouse reminds Ernie of the friendly landlord who rented his father a small farm, while a wood-frame house on a hill finds Ernie reminiscing about good times at an indoor ballroom that was once attached to it.

In Western, the house where Ernie was born stands here, two widows lived over there and this is the house Ernie's father built in 1939 when the family returned to town. The Cedar Rapids Horseman's Club building looks different now than when Ernie's father had it built as an International Harvester farm implement dealership. Girls who lived a mile to the north, up there on a far hill, used to walk this way and accompany Ernie to school. If they were lucky on the walk home the sorghum plant in Shueyville had a sweet treat or two.

In Shueyville, the blacksmith shop is gone, the general store is now somebody's house and the former DX filling station, where Ernie recalls an encounter with traveling gypsies, is now a pizza place. The house his family rented for his father's second farming venture, on the east edge of town, has been updated with plumbing and electricity. The Shueyville High School is today the community center with an addition that makes it both larger and more useful.

In Swisher, this is the house Ernie and Joanne built by referring to a book that explained how to build a house for $3,500 or less. It is a house that allowed them to live the rest of their lives mortgage-free. But there was plenty of hard work here, too, unloading heavy sacks of feed from railroad cars and knowing that wasn't the life Ernie wanted to lead even though he did enjoy being mayor for a while. And, out in the country, west of Swisher, sits the farmhouse his grandparents built and lived in, a house that had been ordered from Sears a century ago and that was delivered in pieces by the CRANDIC railroad.

This is Ernie's early life, before he enlisted in the Army, before he earned an engineering degree at Iowa State University, before he completed his law degree at the University of Iowa and then decided he didn't want to be an attorney. It is just the beginning of half a century in the banking business with moves to Anamosa and Cedar Rapids, a friendship with Cedar Rapids entrepreneur Howard Hall that became more valuable than words can convey, a life based on his mother's philosophy that when you give of yourself it comes back to you twofold.

But, this is not a biography, per se. Sure, it's about Ernie's life. But it's more than that. It's an examination of life in general, the lessons gained and passed on, the idea that we should never stop observing, never stop learning.

"I hope people get out of this that nothing is impossible under the right circumstances," Ernie says. "It is training yourself to know the difference between needs and wants. It is having the right attitude."

This is the second of 88 chapters. In a way, that's one for each year of Ernie's life. But, in another way, since there are 88 keys on a piano, it's a journey of high notes and low notes, a journey down the middle of the road, a journey that began by stuffing cardboard in well-worn shoes and building a soul.

Dave Rasdal

Chapter 3

The Widows Next Door

The first time I remember making any money on my own was about the time I became a teenager. I'd guess it was the seventh grade or eighth grade.

My family had moved back to Western in 1939 when my father's eight-year experiment with farming didn't work out. He became an International Harvester dealer, putting up not only the business' building that is now the Cedar Rapids Horseman's Club, but also our new house that we moved into a couple of years later.

About a block away lived a couple of older women. Maybe they were sisters, or old maids, but at my age I always thought of them as widows. I know they seemed really old. And really nice.

Why, they allowed me to mow their grass. And they paid me for it! A whole quarter.

When the grass grew long enough to mow, I'd grab the old reel-type push mower they kept on hand out behind their house. I remember how it whirred as I'd push it back and forth across their yard. And when I was done, they'd give me some lemonade if it was hot and maybe some candy, too. And then that quarter.

I really think I would have mowed their yard for free. They were so nice. And they needed help. The quarter was such a bonus.

Of course, I was used to working for free on the farm. My older brother, Les, usually helped my dad, so I'd help my mother. Mostly that meant gathering eggs from our chicken house, separating cream from the milk she got from her cows, picking and cleaning fresh vegetables from her garden, tearing up cloth for her loom. We were too poor for me to get an allowance.

Boy, every quarter I earned burned a hole in my pocket.

Luckily, we visited Cedar Rapids at least once a week to deliver my mother's eggs to the Me Too grocery store on 16th Avenue SW and to take cream across the Cedar River to the Wapsi Valley Creamery on Ninth Avenue SE. We'd buy day-old bread at the Peter Pan bakery and always stop at the Old Mill Ice Cream Shop on Third Street SE where I'd spend a nickel for an ice cream cone.

What happened to the 20 cents in change? Why, I saved it. But not for any long term goals. At that age, I didn't have to worry about spending my money on needs. Just wants. And I wanted to make sure I always had money for another ice cream cone the next time we went to Cedar Rapids.

Emma Stanek, Ernie's mother, poses in a field near Shueyville about the time she met and married Joe Buresh.

Chapter 4

My Wise Mother

Hard work and being poor made my mother wiser. It certainly didn't affect her longevity. She cooked everything with lard and still lived to be 97.

My mother was about five and a half feet tall, gained very little weight as she aged and wore glasses later in life. Her hair was always short and tightly curled, turning from dark brown to having flecks of gray to becoming nearly white. While her voice wasn't anything extraordinary, it was always familiar and comforting to me

She was born Emma Anna Stanek on April 2, 1899, on a farm west of Swisher in a house that her parents ordered from Sears, Roebuck and Co. She had two brothers who died at a relatively young age. She worked hard as a girl and it carried on into adulthood, especially after she married my father, Joe Buresh, on June 12, 1921.

I recall my mother talking about the wedding, how it was a small ceremony and that she didn't wear her wedding dress. The roads that day were wet and muddy. She wanted to keep her dress clean for pictures later. She taught me to think ahead, too.

My mother saved pictures all her life and put them into scrapbooks. I have those now and can go back to look at them to bring back old memories.

17

Emma Stanek and Joe Buresh married on June 12, 1921.

I have a lot to say about my mother. Even though she only finished the eighth grade, her principles guided me all of my life. Ever since I could remember, she worked as hard as anyone I've ever known. She never seemed to sit down and relax; she'd always knit while watching TV later in life. When I was young, even before she milked our six or eight cows every morning, my mother was up before the sun preparing for her day. If she left the house it was to work, either cleaning houses for other people or taking her cream, produce, and rugs to market.

My mother baked kolaches all the time. Strawberry and raspberry, peach and cherry, prune and poppy seed. I overloaded on them. I think that's why I'm not a kolache lover today.

So, my mother wasn't perfect. But she was the best role model a boy could have hoped to have while growing up during The Great Depression. Common sense goes a long way toward efficiency. And hard work never hurt anybody.

Chapter 5

My Friendly Father

My father treated his friends better than he treated his family. He was always my father, but he was never my friend.

If he wasn't working on cars, which he did early in my life, or farming the less than adequate land he rented or trying to build his business selling and repairing International Harvester tractors and equipment, he was out hunting, fishing or drinking with his friends. Everybody liked Joe.

Yeah, Joe was jovial and stocky on a five-foot-ten frame and always combed his hair back on top as if he was running into the wind. He enjoyed reading western novels, especially those by Zane Grey. When I look at pictures of him in his younger days, I think he was rather handsome in his World War I uniform when he was in the cavalry. That was a good role for him, since he used horses to farm both before and after the war.

Joseph Frank Buresh was born on a farm near Shuevyville on May 17, 1901. Birthdays weren't a big event in our family. Mom would bake a cake and that was about it. And when it came to my father's work, I pretty much stayed away. He had a tenth-grade education and tried hard to succeed, though he was limited in that regard due to some bad luck. He didn't really want my help as I grew up. He was much closer to my older brother, Les.

Joe Buresh built the J.I. Case building in Western, Iowa, that would later become home to the horseman's club. Note the old gas pumps and the Coca-Cola sign to the left along with some tractors.

I remember one time when Les went out with friends and drank a little too much alcohol. When he came home, boy did my dad give him a going over. But that didn't make a lot of sense. My dad often had too much to drink and that's when he became a different man. He'd celebrate New Year's Eve with his friends at his shop, drinking and playing Euchre to try to win a handful of English walnuts that they used for money.

I saw my father drink too much plenty of times. You hear about someone getting the "snakes," seeing hallucinations, and my dad would get that way. One time I called my uncle, Lou, dad's younger brother who was a teacher and had a hardware store. Uncle Lou came to our house and calmed my dad down.

My father had a temper, too, especially after drinking. I don't recall ever seeing him hit my mother, but he could say some awful things to make her cry. Les and I would argue, like brothers do, and he would pull out the razor strop. He'd smack me on the rear and I remember how it stung. But I recall the threat of it happening again more than I remember any soreness or pain. I don't think he wanted to hurt us; I think he just wanted us to learn a lesson. That was how he did it.

But my dad did try to help the family in ways other than making money. He hunted rabbits and squirrels and raccoons for our table. He took me hunting once, but I couldn't pull the trigger. It was okay for some people, but not for me. He also liked to fish a lot in the Cedar and Iowa rivers. He'd bring home carp and smoke it until it was well done and, really, it was pretty good.

Joe Buresh, Ernie's father, was caught dosing off after a day's work. As an avid reader, it's not surprising he had The Cedar Rapids Gazette on his lap.

Probably the farming background influenced that part of my father's life. He'd also butcher hogs for us, although my mother would be left to cut it up, fry it and store it in fruit jars so we'd have meat through the winter. Sometimes my father would buy a quarter of beef to divide with a friend, but we ate more chicken and pork than we did beef.

My father lived to be 77, which still somewhat surprises me today. He died in 1978 at St. Luke's hospital in Cedar Rapids. He just got sick and died a few days later. I think it was pneumonia. I just couldn't bring myself to visit him there, even though I was in my fifties. My mother didn't say much about his death either way. She was a strong woman. I know she loved him in her own way and for her, after he died, it was simply time to go on with life.

Joe and Emma Buresh pose with the cake celebrating their golden wedding anniversary in 1971.

Chapter 6

My Older Brother

My brother was my father's favorite which, by default, made me my mother's favorite. I suppose that had to do with the four years difference in our ages and the fact my father was farming when I came of age. Les, because he was older, could help on the farm and became my father's right-hand man.

Ernie Buresh, 18 months old, and his brother, Les, who was 6 years old.

I always looked up to my brother. He was a lot harder worker than I ever thought of becoming. He was the best looking member of our family, with a cleft in his chin like my father, which is why I guess my parents decided to have me more than four years later. They didn't know I wouldn't be a beautiful baby, too.

Lester "Les" Frank Buresh was born Feb. 11, 1922. He grew up to be the tallest in our family but he wasn't six-foot tall. He helped both of my parents, but mostly my dad. After high school he worked for Arthur Collins, both at Collins Radio in Cedar Rapids and at the Collins house in far southeast Cedar Rapids. One day he came home frustrated because Mr. Collins bawled him out for not walking flat-footed on the lawn and his heels had dug gouges in the ground. At least that's what Les said.

When World War II came along, Les enlisted to be a pilot. I'm not sure why he didn't become one at the time. He did get into the Army Air Corps, later called the Air Force, as a bombardier on a B-29 in the Pacific Theater based in Okinawa.

Before Les went into the service, he married Doris Krob on Dec. 12, 1942, and she went with him to various training bases. They had three children, Linda, Cynthia and Barbara.

After the war, Les worked in the farm implement business in Cedar Rapids until he bought the International Harvester dealership in Mount Vernon in 1949. He was more successful at it than our father had been. Also, he did become a pilot and bought his own airplane to fly around Eastern Iowa.

As my older brother, Les was always in my corner. He was relieved when I didn't have to go overseas during the war and helped me buy my first bank. In 1960, he cosigned the loan for me to purchase the Farmers Savings Bank in Martelle with Al Morrisey, a wonderful partner. Three years later I talked Les into joining me in the business.

We might have argued as kids, but we never exchanged a harsh word working together later. He never questioned a thing I suggested and always went along with what I said. He'd suggest some things, too, and we'd do some of them. He always said that I was the one who put this all together, so every decision was left up to me. Maybe that's because I had a college education and he didn't.

Les and Doris moved to Mesa, Ariz., after he retired, and that's where he died in 2004. I remember when Les called me to say he'd been diagnosed with cancer. "I have lung cancer," he said, "but it wasn't caused by smoking."

Les smoked ever since he was in the service; maybe earlier, too, I'm not sure. The Army handed out cigarettes like Santa Claus hands out candy at Christmas, but I never took up the habit. I was too tired from marching and drills, so I'd take a little nap while everybody else was lighting up. That saved me.

I think about it now and have no idea how much money I was able to save by not smoking and not drinking. Unknowingly, that helped me financially; it can help anyone. I could never have told my brother that, though. He was his own man.

Chapter 7

My Younger Sister

My younger sister was a surprise. Joan Ellen Buresh arrived Sept. 18, 1939, a year that seemed prosperous to us as a family with a new house, a new business for my father and a new car. She was another gift.

Ernie Buresh with his sister, Joan, in September, 1944.

Being 13 years younger than me, Joan wasn't a big part of my life as I went on to high school. But she became close to my mother as they would go shopping at Goodwill for secondhand clothes and often attended movies together.

Joan had reddish hair and freckles, but otherwise looked a lot like my mother. I recall one time my father made a fuss about

26

buying her new shoes, but I think she got them anyway. My parents were doing a little better by then. And Joan grew up without much, so she appreciated everything. I know she was happy when, during the time I had saved some money in the service, I bought her a second hand bicycle that she could ride around Western.

This two story house in Western, Iowa, became home to Ernie Buresh's family in 1939 before his parents built a new house nearby. This picture was taken several years later.

Since my brother, Les, was in the service, his wife, Doris, and their first daughter, Linda, lived with my parents for a while. As a result, Joan became good friends with Linda and was there when Linda fell into an old concrete cistern on my parents' place and had to be rescued.

In a lot of families, especially when there's such a difference in age between the second youngest and the youngest, that youngest child gets spoiled. That never happened with Joan. She didn't have any advantages at all; in some ways she may have had a tougher childhood than either Les or I had because our parents were older. So it wasn't surprising that after Joan graduated from high school, she moved to Oklahoma to attend college and never again lived in Iowa.

Joan was able to find a great job as an office manager in Oklahoma, married a Texas man, Bill Ratliff, and has now retired with him in Albuquerque, N.M. They didn't have any children.

We only see each other every few years, but we talk frequently on the telephone. I send Joan and Bill Omaha Steaks for Christmas and she sends me her homemade peanut brittle. It's the best peanut brittle ever made, which always fondly reminds me of my mother.

Chapter 8

Generosity's Reward

My mother's favorite philosophy, the one that she based her life on for 97 years, was to treat people like you want them to treat you. The Golden Rule. It was to be generous even when you could least afford it.

"Everything you give away," my mother liked to say, "will come back to you twice over."

We weren't the poorest family when I was growing up. We had neighbors who lived in a sheep shed. I remember the children would come to school with their lunches – just lard plastered between two pieces of rye bread. My lunch wasn't much better, but at least I had meat. And I felt lucky for that.

Just getting by was part of life during The Great Depression. I don't remember ever actually being jealous of what others had. I was just sometimes ashamed at how little I had. I was no angel, either.

I hate to admit it, but I was a bully once in grade school. I would pick on little Frankie Teffer. I would badger him and bat him around with my hands. When he wouldn't react, I'd push him again. I don't know that he ever went to the ground but it was bad. I was a bully and I don't really know why.

I've regretted it all of these years. I would think about it from time to time. I wasn't brought up to treat people like that.

I found Frankie after I became a banker. I called him up and took Frankie and his wife to lunch. We talked about growing up together, about school. I reminded him of the times I'd bully him. I apologized.

Well, Frankie smiled back at me. "I don't remember anything about it," he said.

Frankie forgave me. He thanked me for lunch. And then, later, he came to my bank and opened a checking account.

To this day, I don't know if Frankie really didn't remember that I bullied him or if he chose to be nice about it and act as if he didn't. All I know is that Frankie Teffer didn't deserve abuse. He was brought up to graciously turn the other cheek. He genuinely lived by The Golden Rule.

A belt from the tractor to an elevator lifts straw into the barn on the farm Ernie Buresh grew up on east of Shueyville.

Chapter 9

Landlord Treats

You like Family

The first time I think I realized how poor we were came when my father became a farmer. I was just ready to start school when we moved to a house about a half mile east of Western on ground that my dad rented from Alfred Witousek.

I'm not sure how the arrangement came about, only that it was a big move for us as a family and that the Witouseks were the nicest people you could ever meet. And I thought they were rich.

The house we moved into wasn't much different than the one we left behind in Western. We used kerosene lamps for light and had an outhouse out back. But it seemed different because we were isolated out in the country away from other people.

The Witouseks – Alfred and Emma and their children, Inez and Donald – lived not far away in a beautiful one-and-a-half story brick house. I thought it was a mansion because it was so big. It had electric lights with push button light switches and there was a bathroom inside. I thought they had everything.

Alfred and Emma were in the same pinochle club as my parents, so they were friends. Everybody played a lot of cards during The Great Depression. And I think there was a mutual respect between Alfred and my father. He relied on my dad for his mechanical ability, to help with broken down machinery. Otherwise, Alfred farmed his farm and my father farmed the rented ground.

Even though Inez was my brother's age and Donald was a couple of years older than me, Inez and I became good friends. We'd play cards, mostly rummy, and a new game called Monopoly.

Two other impressions from those days were listening to the radio, to Little Orphan Annie, and sending away for the free stuff, and going to an occasional movie. The picture I always remember is "The Trail of the Lonesome Pine," an early movie shot in color that had feuding and action that kids like.

I had the first real scare of my life in our house out in the country. I woke up one morning and nobody was there. I felt I'd been abandoned and ran up to the Witouseks' brick house all upset because I couldn't find anybody.

My father was probably working and my older brother, Les, was either helping him or at school, and my mother had gone out somewhere. She might have been just around the corner, but at that age you didn't have the sense to just wait for them. You needed the security of your family. Really, you never outgrow that.

Chapter 10

A Doctor's

Prescription for Fun

Our family doctor was more than that. He was a friend and the first man I remember meeting who received respect from everyone in the community. And, as far as I was concerned, he deserved it.

Dr. Wes Netolicky delivered my older brother, Les, and he delivered me. His office was in the back of his house which wasn't far from Buresh School east of Western. And he made house calls whenever anyone got sick.

In the days when most people didn't have much, Dr. Netolicky was doing okay, at least from a kid's perspective. Behind his house was a tennis court and in one of his buildings he had a shuffleboard court. Whenever some of us kids wanted to play, he didn't mind at all.

Somehow I acquired an old wooden tennis racquet – my mother probably found it at a garage sale – and I'd play tennis with some of the other kids, mostly Inez Witousek. She was older and better at it than I was. I was never that good at anything like that. But I do know that sometimes I'd win. She might have let me. That's what good people do.

We also played some shuffleboard but not as much as tennis. I don't think Dr. Netolicky wanted us around THAT much. But he was so good to us. I always remembered that when it came to sharing what you've got with others.

Ernie Buresh, right, takes a break from tennis with Eddie Melsha and Bernice Dvorak.

Chapter 11

A Scrub Tree for Christmas

Every year, when we were poor and living on a farm, my father would go out into a pasture and cut down a scrub Cedar tree for Christmas. I'm sure he believed in Christmas, but I'm also sure he did it for my mother, brother and me. He knew we didn't have a lot of reasons to celebrate.

Once the tree was up, my mother would pop popcorn and get out needles and string. She'd sit down with Les and me to string the kernels together and drape the strings of popcorn around the skimpy branches of the tree.

To finish off the festivities – because we didn't do much for Christmas or birthdays or any other special occasions – my mother would make caramel corn with sorghum molasses and some of her buttery caramels that she wrapped in waxed paper. They would just melt in your mouth.

Even though I knew we didn't have much, I was just like any other kid. I had my wishes, too, and hoped for a present under the tree.

One year I hoped to get a little red wagon so I could kneel in it and push with my other leg. And, what do you know? A slightly rusty red wagon showed up that year.

That made me believe in miracles.

Ernie's grandparents on his father's side, Mary and Frank Buresh in the back row, stand in front of a log cabin home with their sons, Joe (left, front) and Louis in the 1910s.

Chapter 12

Wired for Electricity

By the winter of 1936, one of the snowiest winters if not still the record holder today, we had moved to another farmhouse just east of Shueyville. I'm not sure why, because the ground wasn't much better.

Maybe we moved so I didn't have so far to walk to school. The old grade school, since moved farther back from the road and converted into a house, was a lot closer for me than when I walked to the Buresh one-room school – only three or four blocks instead of three-fourths of a mile. I do know that when I felt like it I could also walk to my grandmother's house which was the next farm south. In fact, that's why that winter sticks out in my mind.

I remember the snow was so high I walked on top of it and onto the roof of my grandparents' barn. I walked all the way up to the peak of the roof. That was a big deal for a boy of about ten, to be able to see the ends of the Earth from the top of a barn.

It was also a big deal when that house was wired for electricity by the Rural Electric Cooperative. Electricity was a wonderful thing when you hadn't had it before. My parents were so glad to get it. They could get rid of the kerosene lamps and the Aladdin lamps, which burned a mantle rather than a wick. They had a flame that didn't flicker and they gave off more light.

The most fascinating device I saw in those days was a mechanical track in a barn on a dairy farm southeast of where we lived. It had baskets that you'd scoop manure into and then you'd operate it to remove the manure from the barn.

We used to ride on that thing to go in and out of the barn. I'm not sure how clean it was. We didn't care. That's what we'd do for entertainment in those days.

Chapter 13

Ernie had a Little Lamb

When you farmed in the 1930s, you did everything. My dad grew corn, oats and hay using horses until he was able to afford a tractor. We raised cows and pigs for livestock. My mother had chickens for the eggs and for eating and later at least one milk cow.

Ernie Buresh clutches one of his mother's chickens on the farm.

If anything smelled horrible to a kid working on a farm, it was the chickens. Cleaning out the enclosed coop of the chicken manure and matted straw was bad enough. But when mother wanted to fix a chicken for supper, she'd dunk it into a boiling pot of water to loosen the feathers. The smell was just awful. It could burn your eyes. I'm glad I never had to do that. I know some people today who won't eat anything that once had feathers because it reminds them of that smell.

I liked birds. In fact, I tried to form a bird-watching club and one of my classmates referred to it as "that crazy bird club." I'd catch wild birds – sparrows, pigeons, robins, gold finches – that hadn't learned to fly yet. I'd feed them, take care of them and let them go pretty soon. I'm not sure if I had any friends in my club or not. It could have been only me. It was just one of those things I tried to organize.

On the farm, my parents treated their animals right. My mother would feed tomatoes to her chickens as a treat and swore it kept them healthy. My dad's treat to his hogs was cooked pumpkin and that became my after-school job as I grew older.

With a corn knife, I'd cut up the pumpkins and dump the pieces into a cooker heated by an outside wood-burning fire. After the pieces had cooked, my dad fed them to the hogs. It was amazing how those hogs fell all over each other to get to those pumpkin parts.

The animals on our farm were never anything more than livestock to me except for the dogs we had around. That is, until I started taking care of a lamb.

I don't remember the lamb's name, but she followed me everywhere. I fed her with a bottle and took care of her. Learning to take care of something that's alive gives kids many valuable lessons as they grow up. It gives them a real sense of worth. Then, one day, my dad said we had to take the lamb to market. That really broke my heart.

Chapter 14

The Day the

Gypsies Came to Town

Popular hangouts for kids in the '30s were gas stations – certainly not the convenience stores of today, but still places where you could buy a candy bar or a bottle of pop and watch cars come and go.

The DX Station in Shueyville became my hangout when we lived in a rented farmhouse just a few blocks east of it. Before I was a teenager, I'd go there with a couple of friends, talk, see other people we knew, watch the station owner, Bill Kopecky, pump gas into the glass cylinder on top of the old-fashioned gas pump and fill up cars as they came and went. The station didn't have any service bay – I guess that's why people like my dad repaired cars in their own garages at home.

One day we were hanging out when a group of gypsies arrived. They weren't dressed much different than a lot of folks in those days, but you could tell they were strangers to the area. Just the way they looked around and acted.

When Mr. Kopecky saw the gypsies, he shooed us out of his store and locked the door behind us. We were a little scared of what might happen but we were more curious than frightened, so we hung around

41

outside. The gypsies and Mr. Kopecky had words through the door but he refused to open it for them. He knew that, if given the chance, the gypsies would fill his little station and steal him blind. If you own a store, you can do what you want, especially when it comes to suspicious customers.

The former DX service station in Shueyville is now a retail establishment.

It wasn't long before the gypsies got the message that they weren't wanted and left. We weren't really sure where they went, but we were relieved that nothing bad happened.

Sometime after that, Emma Witousek, our former landlord's wife, took my mother and me for a ride in the country. She wanted to show us the gypsies' camp.

I'd guess there were a dozen people hanging around campfires built among tents and old parked cars arranged haphazardly in a field. As long as we were inside the enclosed car I felt safe.

When Mrs. Witousek began to leave, her car quit running. It just stopped. I was scared to death. What if those gypsies came to help us? What if they wanted something from us? What if they wanted to take me away?

Then Mrs. Witousek and my mother laughed. Mrs. Witousek started her car and we drove away.

They had just been pulling my leg, sharing a joke at my expense. I didn't think it was funny. Not until I was much older. Not until I realized that was the way people who were poorer than we were lived in those days.

Chapter 15

The Check under a Brick

The two-story house my father built when we returned to Western was the first place I remember that had plumbing. No more ice cold midnight trips to the outhouse in the middle of the winter; no more holding my breath because of the odor that permeated that little enclosed building behind our other houses.

Our new home also had electricity, although this wasn't the first time. I recall my mother changing light bulbs in the house we rented east of Shueyville after electricity was installed.

Our new house, like many in those days, was heated with an oil-burning space heater. If there's one thing that stands out as I came of age in that house, it was watching my father sign a blank check for the oil delivery man and then place it beneath a brick on top of the empty oil barrel.

The delivery man would stop, fill the oil drum, fill out the dollar amount on the blank check and take it with him. Maybe sometimes he'd talk to my father, but he didn't have to. He left us oil that kept us warm and my dad left him a check that was always good.

Honesty in those days was a given. You trusted your friends, your neighbors, the people who worked for you and the people who came by on a regular basis. You could leave your bicycle by the side of the road and nobody would take it, your house unlocked and nobody would come inside unless they were invited, the key in the ignition of your car and it would be there in the morning.

Maybe that's why, in the early days of my banking career, I could look a man in the eye and see that he was honest. A handshake would have been good enough if the paperwork hadn't been required.

It could all probably go back to that check my father left under a brick. Nobody would steal it. A man's word was golden.

Chapter 16

New Cars and Old Cars

For some reason, 1939 was a good year for our family. That's when my father quit farming and moved our family to Western into a temporary house until he built us a new one. It was near the International Harvester farm tractor and implement dealership that he also had built and that would become his business for the next several years.

Les Buresh, in his Army Air Corps uniform, sits on the hood of the 1939 Plymouth he received for high school graduation with an arm around his wife, Doris.

That was the year my parents bought a brand new 1939 Chevrolet. It was also the year my brother, Les, received a brand new 1939 Plymouth as a gift from our grandmother for his graduation. It cost $800.

You might have thought our house was a

new car dealership until you saw my old Ford Model A also parked in the yard. My parents had driven Model A Fords before they bought the new car.

I paid $20 for my car, but I didn't drive it a lot because I had to buy gasoline for it. I remember that gas was 19 cents a gallon. But I wasn't working, not even mowing lawns any more, to earn money, so even a couple of gallons of gas was often out of reach.

I have to laugh. I know my car wasn't good enough to take my girlfriend out in it. It was a junker, but it ran.

I remember filling up at the station in Cou Falls that also had a pool hall. I didn't play pool much because that cost money. But the station attendant was short and he couldn't get the best look at the lines as he'd pump the gasoline up into the glass cylinder at the top of the pump before he put it into my car. I'm sure I always got a little extra gas so that's why I liked to fill up there.

As my mother said, always look for a bargain.

Chapter 17

A Long Walk's Sweet Reward

Soon after we'd settled into our new house in Western, I began high school. It was located a little more than a mile to the south in Shueyville. It closed in the 1960s when the College Community School District was formed and is, today, the Shueyville City Hall and Community Center.

This was the early 1940s and I always walked to school. I didn't have the option to ride a bus; the district didn't have any. It was something I always looked forward to, not only the walk to school but being in class with friends all day and the walk home.

Every morning, Irene and Irma Rigel, who lived about a mile north of Western, walked past our house. They were always on time. You could set your clock by them. And I'd always walk to school with these girls because it was more fun to have company.

The walk home, of course, was always more enjoyable than the walk to school. For one, it was always light out, while you might have to walk in the dark in the morning. It was also the warmest part of the day during the winter. And occasionally – as often as we could – the Rigel girls and I would stop at Bowersox Sorghum Mill where Jim Bowersox was always friendly to us no matter how busy he might be.

Sometimes, we'd watch Mr. Bowersox run some of the cut stalks of sweet sorghum through a set of

47

rollers to squeeze the juice out of them. The juice would run down into these special pans that were simmering over a hot fire. He would use a wooden ladle to guide the cooking sorghum through a maze that was built into the pans so liquid wouldn't burn. And when it became the right consistency, he'd pour the processed sorghum into metal gallon buckets and sell it.

Ernie Buresh (left) has a sack lunch tucked under his arm as he walks to Shueyville High School with George Zalesky.

My mother bought sorghum from the Bowersox mill and used it to make syrup for our pancakes, to coat popcorn for caramel corn and to make hard candy.

Mr. Bowersox was such a nice guy he didn't care if we took a stalk of sorghum for ourselves. He'd even cut it into smaller pieces for us.

And what would we do with a stalk of sorghum? We'd put it in our mouth and suck on it. It was so sweet and made for a pleasant walk the rest of the way home. Thank you to every adult like Mr. Bowersox.

Chapter 18

Bad Shoes Haunt

Again in High School

Even though my mother only finished the eighth grade and my father quit school after tenth grade, they didn't make a fuss when my older brother, Les, graduated from Shueyville High School in 1939.

I followed Les into the same white-frame school building that was larger than any of the others I'd attended. Actually, it wasn't much different than before, only on a higher level.

We had 30 or 31 students in the whole Shueyville High School and all of us would meet for home room first thing every morning in the large room in the middle of the building. When a class was in session, those in attendance would go into one of the two smaller rooms off to the side while the rest of us stayed in the central room.

It seems strange that so many years after having to endure cardboard in my shoes when I started school, that bad shoes would come back to haunt me again.

I played guard on the Shueyville High School basketball team, but we didn't have a gymnasium. We'd go to Swisher and practice at an old dance hall that resembled a barn on the west end of Main Street. It's a house, now. But, in those days, they'd have dances and when they were over the floor would be slick from wax that was applied for the dances. That meant, for basketball, shoes with good traction on the floor were very important.

I slipped a lot because all I had were inexpensive shoes. Elroy Maul, our basketball coach, rode me about that. He said, "You can't play $10 ball with a 50-cent pair of shoes."

The other kids picked that up and teased me about it. I kept playing and figured I was OK because I was wearing No. 11, not No. 13, which I thought would have been very bad luck in those days.

Ernie Buresh (No. 11) poses with his 1941-42 Shueyville High School basketball team. Front row, left to right, are George Zalesky, Ernie, Joe Zalesky, Harold Novotny and A.J. Ziskovsky. Back row, left to right, are Guy Louvar, Bob Zach, the coach, Bob Netolicky and Clarence Netolicky.

One thing I'll never forget is the favorite yell of the Shueyville High School cheerleaders. I'm not sure it would be allowed today, but it's funny to remember. The cheerleaders would shake their pom-poms and shout: "Shueyville High School, you are it! SH for Shueyville and IT for it!"

I also played the trombone at Shueyville High School but I didn't have a case for it. I had to be extra careful carrying that used trombone around so I didn't bend or dent the slide. I also played a little outside of school for the Leonard Reyman Band. It was just a few times for fun. I later became great friends with Leonard.

I do recall that one day, for some reason, we had a high school band concert in North Liberty. Remember, this was the early '40s, so it was a small town, too. Anyway, nobody showed up for our concert. I mean, only three or four people. We had more kids than that in the band.

I wasn't a very good student, but I'm not really ashamed of that. I'd show you my report card if I could find it. But, I never really enjoyed reading and, when you're poor, finding the time to read is a luxury. You're always doing some work or another.

One summer I rode with my brother, Les, to Cedar Rapids to work for Collins Radio. While he knew the founder and owner, Arthur Collins, and often did work for him at his home, I spent all my time in the sheet metal department. I'd use a heavy shear operated by a foot pedal to cut metal for the radio cases. It was hard work and dangerous – I certainly didn't want to lose a finger under that sharp cutting blade.

I think that's part of the reason I decided to transfer to Wilson High School in Cedar Rapids for my senior year of high school. I wanted to get an education so I didn't have to do manual labor. I wanted to go to Iowa State in Ames to become an engineer, maybe even an

51

architect. And I needed more mathematics than Shueyville offered.

By now I didn't have to walk – no more worn shoe leather – because I'd ride with brothers Don and Harold Dvorsky from our homes in Western to Cedar Rapids. This was a great favor from them and I'm not sure that I ever did give them anything in return for the ride. I am eternally grateful, though.

At Wilson, I took mostly math classes. The sheer size of the school was a real eye-opener. There were more kids in one class than we had in the entire Shueyville High School. What bothered me most was not having friends like I did in Shueyville. I made a few new ones but it wasn't the same.

What I really enjoyed was drafting classes. I've never felt I have much God-given talent, except maybe common sense, but I did have a little bit of artistic talent when it came to straight lines. I loved drafting. I probably would have been an architect if other opportunities hadn't come along.

In the spring of 1944, we had high school graduation in the Wilson gymnasium. I wore a rented cap and gown. I don't recall how large the class was, only that a lot of parents came to watch their students graduate.

My parents were not there and I'm not sure why except maybe that, being poor, they didn't want to stand out in such a large crowd.

Remember, this was during World War II. We'd been at war against Japan, Germany and Italy for more than two years.

My graduation was on a Thursday. That Sunday, just three days later, I was taken to Union Station in Cedar Rapids where I boarded a train for Camp Dodge near Des Moines to begin serving my country.

Ernie Buresh wears his cap and gown for a portrait after he graduated from Wilson High School in Cedar Rapids.

A Working Guy

ERNIE BURESH

Chapter 19

In the Army Now

"You'd be better off getting a job at the packing house," my father said as he signed the papers for me to join the Army.

I was only 17 – my eighteenth birthday wouldn't be until October – but I was out of high school and that's when it seemed most kids in those days went out to find a job.

Ernie Buresh (right) poses with his roommate, Bill Cameron, in a photo he sent to his parents. On the back, Ernie wrote: "This is Bill (my roommate) and me. We get along together swell but he is kinda hot tempered."

Being I have a Czech heritage, and that Czech men had been working at the meat packing house in Cedar Rapids, first Sinclair and later Wilson's, since it opened in the 1870s, my dad thought that was the place for me.

Really, I wanted to go to college but I didn't have any money. With the war on, a lot of kids enlisted before they were drafted. My older brother, Les, enlisted and he was stationed in Okinawa in the middle of the Pacific Ocean at the time. I thought that was the way to go, too.

My early experience at Camp Dodge, however, made me wonder. It was embarrassing to stand naked in front of everybody else for "The Short Arm" examination.

But it was even more embarrassing after we were issued our new uniforms and I wore mine through the chow line for the first time. Somebody bumped my tray full of food and splattered gravy all over the front of my uniform. You don't soon forget an embarrassing moment like that.

I completed basic training at Camp Hood in Texas where we marched – actually, we walked our butts off – learned to shoot and crawled under barbed wire while live ammo was being shot across the field right above us.

Once basic was over, I was shipped off to the Port of Embarkation in New Jersey.

Never do I remember my parents showing any concern for me being in the Army. But, while I was there waiting for orders, I received a letter from Les all the way from Okinawa. He was worried about his little brother.

As it turned out, I didn't leave the United States. So many young soldiers – probably because they were very inexperienced – had been losing their lives that the government put a moratorium on sending 18-year-olds into battle.

I have to look back on my service time as one of the best things that ever happened in my life. I didn't have a clue what I wanted to do. It taught me discipline. I also managed to find some maturity.

I was fortunate enough to earn some actual education while I was in the Army. I shipped up to South Dakota State University in Brookings, S.D., for a semester and that's when I decided I wanted to become an engineer. I was also able to finish another semester at Rutgers University.

After my honorable discharge in 1946, I served in the Army Reserves for a few years – the weekend drills and the service training in the summer.

I remember artillery training at Camp Sheboygan in Wisconsin where we lobbed shells into Lake Michigan. That's where I really made friends. A few of us and our wives formed a card club to play five-hundred and had dinner once a month. Our club lasted 50 years. You just never know when meeting someone will lead to a lifelong friendship.

Ernie Buresh, (left) and his brother, Les, wear their uniforms for a family portrait with parents, Joe and Emma, and sister, Joan, in 1946 after they were discharged from the service.

Chapter 20

Observations:

Ernie Leaves Home

Decisions, decisions, decisions.
Life is full of them and nobody knows that better than Ernie Buresh. Up until now, most decisions had been made for him. That's the way it is before you graduate from high school. Then you're on your own.

Who knows where Ernie – or any of us, for that matter – would have ended up if we had followed dad's advice. Sure, we want our parents' input, but we don't need to accept it as gospel. At 18 we have to start thinking for ourselves, acting upon our decisions and taking full responsibility for our actions.

If Ernie had followed his father's advice, there's no telling where he would have ended up. He could have spent his life cutting up hams for a living. But he realized his potential was greater than that.

Maybe Ernie was lucky that his father tried a variety of ventures – auto repair, farming, a farm implement dealership – while Ernie was growing up. Ernie learned early that risk was part of trying to get ahead in life.

He was definitely lucky to have a supportive mother who was not only smart, but had a wealth of common sense.

One of Ernie's favorite expressions is, "It was a no-brainer."

In 1944, joining the Army out of high school was a no-brainer. Most every American male did the same. The United States had been at war for several years and the tide was turning. Patriotism was high. You wanted to be a part of maintaining the freedom our forefathers fought so gallantly to earn and maintain.

Ernie Buresh stands atop the Agricultural Engineering float during a Veisha parade at Iowa State University in Ames. Ernie attended college on the GI Bill and thought his future was in agricultural engineering.

Little did most of these young fighting men and women realize that their service to country would provide them with so much more – a perspective on life, a maturity that comes with being an adult, and the all-important building of lifelong relationships.

In the Army (Marines, Navy and Air Force, too) you made friends and learned to trust them with your life.

You returned the favor. It's what building relationships is all about.

For Ernie, as you'll see in this section, building relationships translated into a marriage that has lasted 65 years, a secure home to raise a family, a sense of belonging in a community and, of course, a wealth of friendships necessary for any successful businessman, especially when you decide to start your own business at a young age.

It's no surprise that Ernie spent 52 years in banking, but that's not what he set out to do after high school.

Oh, sure, one of Ernie's early jobs was as a bank delivery boy. But at that time he had no inclination that banking should become his career.

As Ernie sits and reminisces – as his mind is jolted into recalling memories he hasn't visited for years – it is clear that he is satisfied and comfortable with the early part of his adulthood.

Plenty of growing pains, yes. A couple of false starts, definitely. But, ultimately, overcoming those challenges made for sweet success.

Dave Rasdal

Chapter 21

Messenger Boy

Actually, my banking career began with my honorable discharge out of the service. I was talking some college courses at Coe College in Cedar Rapids and living with my parents in Western and needed to earn some money. There was an opening for a messenger at First Trust and Savings Bank in Cedar Rapids. It was across the Cedar River from Czech Village at the corner of Third Street and Twelfth Avenue SE, a building that I would own decades later.

My job was to pick up bank deposits from businesses that included offices, retail locations like hardware stores and a couple of restaurants. I'd count the money to verify the deposit and drive it back to the bank in a car the bank provided.

It didn't pay a lot, but it was an easy job, a safe one for a kid. If you were doing it today, you'd probably have to carry a gun. Even though I'd been in the service, I wouldn't have done the job if I'd had to carry a gun.

Frank Dvorak, the bank's cashier, was my boss. I learned quickly that you do what the boss wants if you are to maintain a good relationship. Occasionally, I'd stop at Boston Fish to pick up a fish dinner and deliver it to Mr. Dvorak's girlfriend.

Chapter 22

The Love of My Life

I met Joanne, my wife to be, on a blind date. I went to a lot of dances in the late 1940s – it was the thing to do after the war. My brother, Les, lived in Mount Vernon at the time and his wife had a good friend from Onslow. That friend told my brother who told me about this cute girl from Onslow.

It was all arranged. The spring of 1949. Les' wife, Doris, had showed Joanne Paulsen a picture of me and she agreed to go out even though she was dating someone else at the time. On this certain night I drove to Mount Vernon and picked her up for our date at the DanceMor Ballroom in Swisher.

Joanne Paulsen (right) and her younger sister, Jane, ride their tricycles in Onslow, Iowa, where they grew up. Joanne would marry Ernie Buresh with Jane as her maid of honor.

By now I'd graduated from college and was working for a living. I had used the GI bill to attend Coe College in Cedar Rapids for a semester while living with my

64

parents in Western and then I transferred to Iowa State University in Ames. In 1948 I earned a degree in agricultural engineering.

Ernie Buresh holds his diploma as he stands between his parents, Emma and Joe Buresh, after he graduated with an agricultural engineering degree at Iowa State University.

More surprising than me graduating – I was never a very good student – was that my parents and aunt and uncle came to the ceremony. Even more surprising was that my father gave me $10. The dollar amount didn't matter. He rarely gave me anything. It was more important that he took the time to come to my graduation in Ames.

Ernie Buresh in his college days at Iowa State University in Ames.

My first job was selling dairy barn manure cleaners for Clay Equipment Company from Cedar Falls. I traveled in Illinois to work with dealers who sold our equipment. The mechanical cleaner ran by electric motors and would scape manure out of a gutter behind the cows and transport it out of the barn.

At first I was just responsible for working with farmers to ensure that the installation of the equipment met their satisfaction. Not long after that, though, I was expected to sell the equipment, too. I quickly learned that wasn't my forte.

I'm no salesman. Maybe that's a talent you're born with. I wasn't. In sales, you may not worry about whether you're telling the exact truth or not and I can't do that. I'm not sure if I was fired from that job or if I quit – it was probably a mutual parting of the ways. I know that if I didn't live up to expectations for a job, it made me uneasy.

I think about my banking career later. When somebody said, "I promise to pay," you had to believe them. But I put just as much emphasis on trying to be sure this was the right thing for them to do and that they could do it. If the reason they wanted the money was right, they'd pay back the loan and be happy about it.

My second job was a research project for the United States Department of Agriculture in Marshalltown. I studied demand and diversification of electricity on farms. The RECs – Rural Electric Cooperatives – were relatively new at the time so it was for them, mostly.

The point was that I had been working. I was making some money. I could afford to take a girl out.

Joanne Paulsen graduated from Onslow High School in 1947, a couple of years before she met Ernie Buresh.

I was looking forward to the date until Joanne nearly canceled it. I wondered if things would work out. She was a student at Cornell

College in Mount Vernon and had been on a geology field trip all day to see the colored sands near McGregor and the Mississippi River. She was tired and sunburned. But, somehow, she went anyway.

Who knows what would have happened if Joanne had stayed home that night. Maybe we would have met later. Maybe we would never have met at all.

As far as I remember, we had a good time. She wasn't as experienced at dancing as I was and had to be home early because of the curfew at her dorm and chapel service the next morning.

When I called her up later for other dates, I only suggested dancing a few times. But, we've been married for 65 years and counting. We've been doing our own dance. And you never know. A single day, when you least expect it, can change your life forever. Be ready and willing to take the leap.

Chapter 23

The Bribe to the Bride (and Groom)

Be practical, not extravagant.

That might have been the first lesson my parents taught me when it comes to money. After all, they didn't have any. But it's advice I've followed all of my life. And it really hit home when Joanne and I decided to get married.

Don't ask me when I first met my wife's parents, Erma and George H. Paulsen – he liked to write it Geo. with the period. I just know that I was impressed by him for two reasons – he was as handsome as any man I'd ever met and he was the cashier (with a financial interest) at the Onslow Savings Bank. I have to think he thought differently of me.

First, I didn't have any money when I was courting his daughter which meant I didn't have my own car. I'd drive my Clay Equipment company car or had to find a ride every time I went to Onslow to see Joanne.

I asked Joanne to marry me when we were in the car, on the way to a movie, I think. I didn't make a big deal about it; I just gave her a diamond ring and she said yes. I didn't ask her father for permission, either, for her hand in marriage, like I should have. That's what an idiot I was. What you see is what you get. Nothing more, nothing less.

Joanne told her parents we planned to marry. They told her they thought she was too young, that they wanted her to finish college first. She was 19 and I was 23, not exactly that young in those days. Actually, I think they didn't want their daughter to marry me, but they weren't going to tell her that. Instead, they gave their approval and wished her luck.

George Paulsen, Joanne's father, about the time he gave Joanne and Ernie $1,000 not to have a big wedding.

Then, Mr. Paulsen took his daughter aside and gave her a proposition. If we didn't have a big wedding, one we expected him to pay for, he would give us $1,000. This was 1949. That's about $10,000 in today's money.

Apparently Joanne's parents knew that I'd been in several weddings for friends, either dressed to the nines or wearing my Army uniform. They probably assumed we'd want a big wedding, too. But when Joanne told me about her father's offer, it was a no-brainer. We needed the money. We weren't going to have a big wedding anyway.

Joanne and I exchanged vows at the Little Brown Church in Nashua on Thanksgiving Day, Nov. 24, in 1949. Her younger sister, Jane, drove us up there on a rainy, sleeting day and stood up for Joanne. My friend from Iowa State, Chuck Brandt, was my best man. I wore a regular brown suit and Joanne had purchased a simple brown dress and jacket from Martin's, a woman's shop in Cedar Rapids, for the ceremony. Joanne had the $1,000 in her account by then. Her corsage was an orchid.

We did have a wedding dance that night at the CSPS Hall in Cedar Rapids. We laugh about it now, but we had nothing at the time. We had the dance because you can't expect to get any presents if you don't invite people to some kind of wedding event.

We hired Marlin Peterson, "The Singing Farmer," for our entertainment. He sang "I Love You Truly" when we came into the hall. I think I gave him a bottle of aftershave as a thank-you.

We didn't have much of a honeymoon then. We spent that night at the Roosevelt Hotel in Cedar Rapids, then went to her parents' house in Onslow for the gifts before driving to Chicago for a weekend stay at the Hamilton Hotel. We also ate a fancy dinner at the Berghoff Restaurant where we were served by male waiters.

We didn't take our real wedding trip until the following year and then it was to the Black Hills and Yellowstone National Park with my mother and my younger sister. The more the merrier, I guess. Life was all about family.

Anyway, Joanne left Cornell College so she could be with me. Our first home together was a $35 a month walkup apartment in a private home in Marshalltown. We shared the bathroom and a refrigerator with a nurse who lived in the other upstairs apartment.

Sunday nights we'd go downstairs to the landlord's apartment for popcorn and homemade fudge. That was usually after we had spent the weekend at her parents' house in Onslow doing laundry and getting some free food, then picking up milk and eggs in Western that my mother would give us.

We were happy. We had most of the $1,000 left. We had faith that our lives together wouldn't always be this way.

Years later, Joanne and Ernie Buresh visited the Little Brown Church near Nashua where they were married in 1949.

Chapter 24

How to Build a

House for $3,500

In many parts of the country after World War II, tract homes became all the rage. Returning GI's needed a place to live and they filled these new homes as fast as construction companies could build them. But that wasn't the case in my old neck of the woods – Western, Shueyville and Swisher. And when my contract job at the Department of Agriculture ended, my new wife and I needed to find a place to live.

It was 1950. We decided to move from Marshalltown to Swisher because that's where my grandmother lived. I'm not exactly sure how it came about – maybe it was her wedding present to us – but she gave us a building lot in northeast Swisher.

My grandmother, Barbara Stanek, had given my brother, Les, a brand new Plymouth when he graduated from high school in 1939. I didn't think I was going to get anything and that was OK. I was just happy for him with the car because he needed it then. I was in the Army three days after I graduated so I didn't need a car after high school.

But now that we had this piece of property, we had to decide exactly what to do with it.

Joanne and I picked up a book about building a house for $3,500 or less. I'm sad because in all the moves we've made since, the book has disappeared. I'd sure love to have it.

But, after a little research, I learned the book was called "Your Dream Home: How to Build it for Less than $3,500" by Hubbard Cobb. It sold more than a million copies in 1950, so we weren't the only ones who had the same idea.

Maybe I was inspired by the fact my father had built the house for us in Western a decade earlier. But I think I was more motivated because of the story my Grandmother Barbara had told about the Sears & Roebuck house her family had built a couple of miles west of Swisher. It still stands today with the separate summer kitchen out back where my grandmother used to cook huge meals for the threshing crews that came in every fall.

The two-story farmhouse built by Ernie Buresh's family more than a century ago was ordered from Sears & Roebuck. Note the summer kitchen off to the right.

The Sears house was ordered from the catalog and delivered by the CRANDIC Railroad to Swisher. From there the pieces were loaded onto hayracks pulled by horses and taken to the building site where it was put together by the family and neighbors. The way they described it, the whole thing was quite an operation.

Joanne and I didn't have any money to order a house that would be that easy to build. We had to do it the old-fashioned way, to build a house as we went along when we could come up with the money. That's why the book we picked up, which had illustrations and suggestions for everything from deciding on a floor plan to securing financing, helped us out.

We did have some money, so I was able to begin the house while I decided what I'd do for a living. I talked to Filbert Vondracek at Swisher Lumber and Feed about our plans to build the house. He was more than happy to help. In fact, as long as we agreed to buy all of our supplies from him, he offered us a place to live rent-free. He owned a brand new spec house that was empty, so we moved in as a contractor dug our new basement.

Once we had the hole in the ground, I dug the trenches for the foundation footings and made sure the concrete was poured correctly for them. I'd never laid concrete block, so I hired that done, too, but I worked hard in the basement to mix the mortar in the old "mud box" for the mason to secure each block in its place.

It was so very hot that year that I never stopped sweating. The foundation was 50 feet long and 24 feet wide, so it took us several days to finish that part of the project.

One day, while I was still working on the foundation, I took off my glasses because they kept slipping down on my nose. I laid them down somewhere and, before I knew it, they were buried in the poured concrete foundation. I needed a new pair of glasses.

Also, I needed a job. With financial help from my new father-in-law – it helped that he was a banker – I borrowed money for the first time in my life to start Swisher Farm Supply, a feed business that we set up in the new basement.

My agreement with Filbert was that we'd move into our house as soon as we could, so we finished one end first. I'm eternally grateful for his generosity which shows what I've known and believed all along – the importance of building solid relationships.

The house Ernie Buresh built in Swisher had recently been completed when this picture was taken in the 1950s.

Our first house demonstrates just how these relationships spill over in entrepreneurial ways. I loved my grandmother and she gave us the land. Filbert became a lifelong friend. My father-in-law was a lifesaver for giving me business loans.

Any successes I've had in my life were primarily a result of people like this who worked with me.

I'll never forget moving day. We had so little to move, just our clothes and some old used furniture, but we were going to our own house. It was a dream come true.

It was a new house, even if all that we'd finished at the time was a bedroom, the kitchen and a small living area with a table and two chairs upstairs and the bathroom and shower in the basement. We would finish the rest of the house in the next couple of years, again, as we had the money to do the work.

A very strange coincidence – and life is full of them – occurred when we drove to Anamosa for a big yard sale.

We bought a convertible sofa, one that turned into a bed. It cost us a quarter. As I recall, it wasn't very good for sitting on or sleeping in, but we didn't use it very long. I know we never slept on it at night.

That yard sale was on North Ford Street in Anamosa. In about a decade we would move onto that very same street after we sold our first house and moved into our second.

Chapter 25

My first business:

Swisher Farm Supply

As the first stage of our house for $3,500 or less neared completion, I thought about what I wanted to do for a living. I had been lucky to find a part-time job – probably as a result of my work with the United States Department of Agriculture – teaching new farming methods to farmers who lived in the Oxford area. Of course my degree in agricultural engineering helped, too.

But, the odd thing about that was, the students knew more about farming than the instructor. I'd never farmed in my life; I'd only seen my father struggle at it. But this was a government program. The farmers got some money to go to school and I had a job. It was beneficial to all of us.

My contact with farmers prompted me to start a feed business out of our new basement. Filbert Vondracek sold feed from his lumberyard, but I didn't really consider that I was competing against him. I sold Kent feed and had the opportunity to meet Gage Kent, the Muscatine man who had started the business.

I was pleasantly surprised how my new business, Swisher Farm Supply, grew, and how I didn't mind at all beating the bushes to find new customers. I thought I didn't like sales from my experience with Clay Equipment. But, when you work for yourself and you see the results, it's a little different; when you've got a note at the bank, it's a little different.

I'd borrow money from Joanne's father and pay it back. It was never more than $1,000 at a time, but that was plenty of money in those days. I worked hard to pay it back early every time.

Ernie Buresh (center), owner of Swisher Farm Supply in the mid-1950s, stands between a Kent Feed sales representative (left) and Bob Olson while Frank Pegum sits behind the wheel of the delivery van. Olson and Pegum worked at the store while Ernie earned a law degree at the University of Iowa.

Our basement wasn't big enough for the business so I leased the old CRANDIC Railroad Depot in Swisher.

My feed came in by rail so that made it easier lugging around those 50-pound bags.

Of course, with the growth I experienced, Swisher Farm Supply also sold seeds and then fertilizer which came in 80-pound bags.

Ernie Buresh visits with Marie (Mrs. Carl) Luettjohann and her daughter, Gae (upper right), at their farm in the mid-1950s when he owned Swisher Farm Supply.

There were times I'd work myself dead tired, selling and loading feed for cattle, hogs, sheep and chickens; selling and loading DeKalb seed corn and seeds for alfalfa and soybeans; lugging those big bags of fertilizer. I'd also make deliveries in an old panel truck that I had painted with "Swisher Farm Supply."

I made good money, we finished our house and we began a family. But I knew I couldn't work that hard, physically, for the rest of my life.

Chapter 26

Along Come the Girls

We'd been married for a couple of years and had talked about starting a family. But it wasn't anything we actually planned or worked at doing – when it happened, it happened.

Joanne likes to tell the story about a visit to my parents' house in late 1951. She said that she'd not felt well the evening before – a little sick to her stomach. The Witouseks, my dad's landlord for his first farm, happened to be visiting. Emma Witousek looked at Joanne and smiled. "Maybe you're pregnant," she said.

Wendy Sue came along April 11, 1952, at St. Luke's Hospital in Cedar Rapids. Early that morning Joanne's water broke. I wouldn't say I was nervous, but I was thankful I could be there and drive to the hospital. It was so early all the traffic control lights in Cedar Rapids were flashing yellow and there weren't any police cars out, so not having to stop and being able to drive faster than the speed limit, a

regular habit of mine, meant we arrived at the hospital in no time.

The nurses took Joanne away and a doctor told me to sit down and relax. When people say sit down, I sit down. And it was a long wait because Wendy wasn't born until that afternoon.

We named her Wendy because we liked the radio broadcaster, Wendy Warren. Sue just seemed natural as a middle name, only Wendy didn't care much for it as she grew up. Now she just uses her middle initial.

Two-and-a-half years later I wasn't able to make it to the hospital for the birth of Sandra Jane. That was Oct. 14, 1954, and I was in my first year of law school. Joanne's mother took her to St. Luke's and then cared for Wendy while Sandy was born. I made it there as soon as I could.

Having a family was wonderful but it also became very clear that my responsibilities, my priorities, would center around what I could do to provide a good life for my family. That's why I'd decided to become a lawyer.

Both girls were smart; I'd say smarter than average, but so would most parents about their children.

Wendy was a gifted little girl – she talked early, had a great vocabulary by the time she was two, was always well-mannered and neat and learned cursive writing soon after she started school. At first she wasn't sure about having a little sister, but she was good to Sandy.

My Grandma, Barbara Stanek, who had given us the property for the house and who lived next door in Swisher, was a big help with the girls. She had a large vegetable garden and taught them how to take care of it. She also grew flowers. The girls would pick Lily of the Valley bouquets to give to their mother.

The girls also loved to play in the playhouse I built for them in Swisher. So, actually, I built two houses there. We moved the playhouse to Anamosa later. Wendy has it today, behind her home in Cedar Rapids.

Sandy Buresh (left) appears awestruck by her second birthday cake in 1956 as her family, parents Ernie and Joanne, and older sister, Wendy, anticipate the celebration.

Sandy was small at birth – just over five pounds – and her feet and hands seemed tiny. Doctors performed a couple of tests on her and she seemed fine. But later, she was found to have a heart murmur, a septal defect, which meant there was a hole in her heart between the left and right ventricles. We were told to just keep an eye on her.

By nine months, Sandy still was not able to crawl. Doctors at University Hospitals in Iowa City – I'll never forget the kindness and gentleness of Dr. Monty Lawrence as he checked Sandy's heart and placed his large black thumb on her tiny white chest – told us her weak heart had kept her body from getting the energy it needed. Exhaustion made it difficult for her to eat properly.

Sandy hadn't developed the muscle tone to stand up. We didn't know it then, but her heart would be a problem for the rest of her life.

Soon, after more tests, we took Sandy to a cardiologist at Children's Memorial Hospital in Chicago. In the 1950s it was one of the best places in the country for children's hearts. I remember the size of the heart monitors they had – like computers, they were a lot bigger then than they are now.

Our trips to Chicago became regular. Every six months we'd drop Wendy off at my mother's house, drive to Marion and board a train for Chicago. We were lucky to have some insurance, but we really didn't have much money. We'd stay at McCormick Seminary where we could get a room for very little cash. The cafeteria was reasonable, too.

By now Sandy had learned to walk, but she didn't run very well and ran out of gas easily. As she learned to talk, a speech problem also became evident.

But doctors in Chicago and at University Hospitals in Iowa City were both encouraging and optimistic.

They helped us set aside most of our worries – but not all of them.

Chapter 27

We Bought the Farm

In 1955, Joanne and I had barely finished our house and we had two daughters. I ran my Swisher Farm Supply business with her help and that of a full-time assistant I'd hired. I was attending law school in Iowa City, a good half-hour away from Swisher in the days of two-lane highways, and many of my classes ran late in the day. We had no idea what kind of expenses we might face with our younger daughter's heart. And then we went out and bought a farm.

Yes, we bought a farm.

It was a 120-acre farm (actually 118 acres because a small acreage had been broken off of it) west of Shueyville.

My father-in-law, George Paulsen, the Onslow banker who had helped me finance the start of my feed business, wasn't very happy, to say the least. He thought I was too young to know any better – I was only 28 – and he didn't want to have anything to do with it. He knew I wasn't a farmer.

Why buy a farm?

I don't know. It seemed everybody else had one.

Two old maids lived in this old dilapidated farmhouse and rented out the tillable land. It wasn't a very good farm, not unlike those my father had farmed, but I thought it could make some money. I offered the women $10,000 for their farm and told them they could live in the house rent free. I promised to add plumbing to it and fix it up. They accepted.

We secured a loan from the Federal Land Bank at four percent interest. I don't remember what the payments were because I didn't have to make them very long.

We were able to secure a good tenant for the farm land. Fellow law school students came out to help clean up some of the timber for free meals. Joanne would fix them hot dogs. And there'd been all of this talk about the Cedar Valley Expressway, a four-lane highway connecting Cedar Rapids and Iowa City.

Traffic moves along I-380 behind the contoured ground of the farm Ernie Buresh bought 60 years ago near Shueyville.

Well, it wasn't long before the Iowa Department of Transportation came knocking on our door. They needed 11 acres of the farm for their new highway that would eventually become Interstate 380. They'd pay us $1,000 an acre.

Once we received that $11,000 check from the department of transportation, we paid off the $10,000 note and had a nice little profit. We also had 107 acres, free and clear, in our name.

Joanne and I have owned that farm for more than half a century. I was lucky, I guess. You never know how something like that might work out.

You could say we bought the farm at just the right time.

Chapter 28

Why Not Become a Lawyer?

When I told my wife I thought I'd like to become a lawyer, Joanne laughed at me.

"You can't become a lawyer," she said. "You don't like to read."

She had a point. But it wasn't that I didn't like to read. It's just that it put me to sleep. Like my mother, who always seemed to be knitting something, I was used to keeping my hands and my mind busy all the time.

Ernie Buresh stands in front of his Swisher home after earning his law degree from the University of Iowa.

I hired a man full time to help with Swisher Farm Supply and took the entrance exam for law school at the University of Iowa. When I passed, I began my daily treks to Iowa City along Highway 218. That was in 1954.

Needless to say, this became a hectic time in my life but I could handle it. I wasn't yet 30. Joanne and I finished our house – she was pregnant with our first child while she pounded nails into the subfloor and helped with the feed business in the basement. Joanne gave birth to our first daughter, Wendy, in 1952, and to our second, Sandy, in 1954. I worked full time at the feed business. And I did get my reading done.

At the University of Iowa, fellow students caught wind of my occupation. They referred to me as "Feeds, Seeds and Deeds."

I found law school challenging and interesting. The most interesting thing was that one of my professors was Sandy Boyd, who would later become president of the University of Iowa. We laughed because he was new to the position and I'm older than he is. I learned a lot from him in school and continued to learn from him as the years went by. We remain close friends to this day.

Law school and the family were keeping me busy enough and we'd had a really good year with the feed business – I think I made more than $10,000 – so we sold Swisher Farm Supply in 1956 to Liness and Mary Littrell of Iowa City. He had experience since his parents owned the chicken hatchery in Iowa City.

I graduated from law school in 1957 and passed my boards on the very first try. Another pleasant surprise. So I set up a little office in our basement, the same basement where the feed business began. I thought it would bring me luck.

I never was very busy as an attorney. People from town came in to see me with questions about small things. That made me scratch my head. All they needed to do was think a little bit about their situation, use a little common sense and work out their problems themselves.

It didn't make sense for me to bill people for something as simple as that. But I guess common sense is anything but common. And I knew right then I couldn't be a lawyer. I couldn't charge people for something I didn't think was chargeable.

Chapter 29

Community Service

If you own a business in a small community and expect local people to buy from you, you've got to give something back. You've got to become a part of the community. It's important to take the time to serve it.

Obviously, this is a way to build relationships that can help you down the road. But it's also the right thing to do.

I have to laugh. I preach the importance of developing relationships, but you can't expect too much from them, either. When I owned Swisher Farm Supply, a frequent visitor was Cal Wagner, an area highway patrolman. He'd often stop in the mornings to grab a free cup of coffee and talk for a few minutes, but I don't think our friendship ever kept me from getting a speeding ticket.

In Des Moines once I ran into Jack Fulton, the safety commissioner who was in my law school class at Iowa, and complained about a speeding ticket I didn't think I deserved. I asked him to look into it. His reply was, "Oh, I already know about that. I looked it up on the computer. You come up as a habitual offender."

I didn't have any ground to stand on. I've had a lot of speeding tickets. I even got onc from the new speed cameras on Interstate 380 in Cedar Rapids. My mother drove fast, too. Maybe I inherited it.

Or, maybe I was just always in a hurry because I kept myself busy.

In the 1950s, when I had the feed business and a new family, when I'd finished up building my house and was attending law school at the University of Iowa, I also found the time to serve the community of Swisher on the school board and as mayor.

When it comes to the school board in a small town, there aren't too many people anxious to do that job. For me it wasn't only helping out the Swisher school district – it only had an elementary school since older kids went to Cedar Rapids – but it was a matter of curiosity. I wanted to see how the school operated. I only served one term because I didn't find it that interesting.

As I look back, I think schools are very inefficient in their operations. I'm not sure you can do much about it. Part of the problem is the board and the administration are spending somebody else's money. They don't spend it like it's their own. This problem also hinders other parts of government and the efficiency of some non-profits as well.

For some reason Swisher had a vacancy for mayor and needed to find someone to finish the term. I decided to run and faced off against Bob Ross, a good friend then and for years after that.

Now Swisher is a strong Czech community – probably stronger in those days – and I couldn't be more Czech. Buresh comes from the Czech surname, Bures.

Anyway, a friend told me he overheard a conversation at the Post Office between two women who obviously had a Czech heritage. One of them said to the other, "I'm not voting for that American."

I became mayor even though I didn't campaign at all. I know I didn't spend any money to get elected. And the first term was short so I ran again and was elected for the next full term.

While I wanted to serve the community, I quickly learned how it's time-consuming work for little reward. You had monthly meetings and got paid maybe $2. It wasn't worth the number of phone calls – mostly about loose dogs, boundary line disputes, the roads needed to be fixed, the streetlight on the corner was out. You do the best you can, but it seemed that no matter what you did, somebody wasn't happy.

I will say it was the worth the time I spent doing it, but I quickly learned that the last thing I wanted to be was a politician.

Later, as I owned banks, I implemented a policy that nobody in my employ could be on the school board or the local government. No matter what you'd do, somebody wouldn't agree with the way you'd vote. They'd get mad enough to close their account at the bank. You were never going to escape that.

You might think that seems petty, both from my perspective and from the way customers acted. But it's more than pettiness. It's the way too many people try to influence other people.

It's not right, but it's the way they want to get you to change your mind even after it's too late; it's the way they want to punish you for not thinking like them in a matter that has nothing to do with your business.

It's one of those rare situations where you can't come out ahead no matter what you do.

Chapter 30

Into Banking

When practicing law wasn't for me, I needed to find a new occupation. I had admired my father-in-law, George Paulsen, since I'd met him. The fact that he made a living at a bank intrigued me.

Anyway, one thing led to another and I began what would become a 52-year banking career in 1958 when I joined the trust department at Merchants National Bank in Cedar Rapids. George had worked with a variety of people at Merchants, so that opened the door. But, with my recent background in agriculture and a law degree, I also was perfectly qualified for the position.

My role was to manage property that the bank held in trust. I would go out in the field and negotiate leases, make sure farmers were using the latest farming techniques and help oversee the management of cattle when the trust was a partner with a livestock-raising tenant.

I got along pretty well from the start. I'm an early riser. Farmers like to get up early – or have to if they've got dairy cattle. I can still get up at four in the morning and not worry about it.

At the time, I parked in an old building that was converted into a parking ramp. It was a block and a half from the bank. I'd be there by seven in the morning, if not earlier, and would run into a few other people, including business owners, who wanted to get a good start on their days. In the bank, the only people I'd run into that early were the custodians. Everyone else would arrive by eight.

I was amazed at how working in Cedar Rapids enabled me to meet so many influential people in a very short time. In the parking ramp I'd often see Morris Sanford, owner of the large stationery/book store. We became friends through the years because of our early morning arrivals.

I'd guess that I met about three-fourth of the lawyers in Cedar Rapids because they all seemed to be working with trusts, estates and wills. If I had any questions, any hesitation about anything at all, I could easily turn to my boss, Russell Hess. He'd been in charge of the bank's trust department for years and could answer all of my questions or find someone who could.

Early friendships at the bank with Forbes Olberg and John Hamilton introduced me to the benefits of investing. Forbes, a long-time employee in the trust department, and John, who become president of Merchant's National Bank while I was there, partnered with me to form JEFCO – John, Ernie, Forbes Company.

In our first venture, we bought a farm in Jones County – 180 acres along Highway 64 between Anamosa and Wyoming. This was in the heart of Grant Wood Country, not far from the Antioch Church and the school where the famous artist grew up as a child.

I had been to Jones County before but, somehow, owning land there brought it closer to my heart. This was the beginning of Jones County becoming a huge part of my family's life for more than half a century since.

JEFCO also bought some bank stock and we managed to make some good money.

But, after three or four years, we dissolved the corporation. Forbes wanted the farm and John wanted cash, so I took the bank stock.

My early years at Merchants National Bank – I would work in the trust department for seven years – also endeared me to the people who owned, operated and worked in small community or county-wide banks. That exposure prompted me to purchase the bank in Martelle in 1960 and Citizens Savings Bank in Anamosa two years later.

Chapter 31

Howard Hall's Influence

Tops among the acquaintances made early in my banking career was Cedar Rapids businessman and philanthropist Howard Hall.

It was the late 1950s when Forbes Olberg, a co-worker in the trust department at Merchants National Bank, introduced us. It seemed Howard needed someone to help him turn around City National Bank which had not been doing as well as he thought it should.

Howard Hall, Cedar Rapids industrialist and philanthropist, plays with the pet lion he kept at his Brucemore estate in Cedar Rapids.

Before long, Howard had me come to Brucemore, his mansion on First Avenue East in Cedar Rapids, for one-on-one consultations. His wife, Margaret, would make sure her cook fixed us wonderful lunches and we'd have them in the formal dining room. Howard had founded City National Bank with a group of others and was the principle stockholder. I guess being in the dining room made the meetings more formal.

But City National, as anyone with knowledge about the history of Cedar Rapids knows, was just the tip of the iceberg for Howard. He'd built up Iowa Steel and Iron and Iowa Manufacturing Company that made rock crushing equipment for the building of roads. He contributed immensely to the community and had recently seen the opening of the Hall Radiation Center (1957) for the treatment of cancer.

As we turned City National around, I became a member of the board and, in the 1960s, president. That was just like Howard – he rewarded people who helped him out.

Even after talking to Howard only two or three times, you couldn't help but be impressed by him. It was amazing how somebody with his position in business and his reputation could turn out to be such an ordinary and friendly person. I immediately realized he had a unique ability in handling relationships with people, whether they be employees, friends or competitors.

Mrs. Hall was the same way. She was a great woman, unimpressed by everything she had, even by her position in life and her role in the future of Cedar Rapids.

My wife, Joanne, helped solidify our friendship with the Halls because she grew up in Onslow – the same town where Howard was raised.

Joanne's father, George Paulsen, the cashier at the bank in Onslow, knew Howard for his "calf" money. That was the money Howard made when he sold a calf he'd raised as a youngster. I don't think he ever touched that money, just let it collect interest. I know he later started a scholarship fund that rewarded the top student at Onslow every year. And he liked to tease

Joanne about their hometown by calling her "Miss Onslow."

As our friendship grew, the Halls would have us out to their stone cottage on a bluff overlooking the Cedar River at The Palisades near Mount Vernon. That's where Joanne first met Howard and Margaret.

We would go to University of Iowa football games together. After the game, Joanne and I would drive to the cottage to start the fire in the fireplace to warm it up while Howard and Margaret would go to Brucemore to pick up the food and their dogs for the cottage. We'd often grill steaks.

Early in our friendship, Howard called one day and said he wanted us to visit him in Florida. I asked when and he said, "Tomorrow." When I hemmed and hawed about the logistics, he insisted we take Delta Airlines, the best airline in his opinion, and that was that.

Ernie Buresh, center, relaxes between Margaret and Howard Hall as they take a ride on the Halls' yacht off Marathon, Florida, in March of 1971.

We flew to Miami and checked into the Sea View Hotel at Miami Beach at Howard's insistence to relax for a day or two to unwind and get acclimated to Florida before we went to their home. We always stayed in the Halls' permanent suite on the seventh floor of the hotel with a gorgeous view of the Atlantic

99

Ocean. We dined there, spent time at the private cabana right on the beach, and relaxed.

The private island owned by Howard and Margaret Hall sits off the coast of Marathon, Florida, in the heart of the Florida Keys. The docks shown in the lower part of this picture postcard belong to the Coast Guard.

After a day or so at the hotel, we spent another four or five days at the Halls' home in Marathon, Florida, on their private island, Palm Island. A Coast Guard station was near the island and a causeway led to it. The Halls had built up the island with a sea wall around it and put only three buildings on it – their home, the guest home where we stayed and a home Howard built for his sister, Irene Perrine.

Even though Howard and I conducted some business back home by phone, business wasn't the purpose of our trips. It was just to relax. We had stone crab and beer for lunches, ate at nice restaurants in the evening, and just enjoyed each other's company.

Soon, Howard was calling me most every night, sometimes fairly late. The phone would ring and he'd say, "I bet you're in bed." Even if I was, I'd say, "Oh no, no," and we'd talk about whatever was on his mind.

I couldn't begin to cover all of the great advice Howard gave me through the years.

There was one time I was asked to be on the Iowa Board of Regents. Being flattered, I probably would have taken it if I hadn't talked to Howard first. He said it would be a waste of time, that any time you'd make a decision, there was going to be somebody who didn't agree with you. You're better off spending time on your own ventures, he said. It reminded me of my time as mayor in Swisher.

Howard also wasn't big on publicity. I always remember that he said, "Don't get your name in the paper – not even in the obituaries."

Joanne and I knew Howard for the last 12 years of his life – he died in 1971 – and Margaret for another 10 years until she died in 1981. They were the most gracious people you'd ever meet. We were at their death beds shortly before they each passed away.

The day before Howard died, I sat in a chair in his room and he was in bed. He motioned for me to sit at the end of his bed. Then he told me, "Don't ever call George Foerstner. Let him call you."

George was the founder of Amana Refrigeration which grew to become a huge manufacturer of refrigerators and other appliances with Howard's help. George was in charge of the company for decades and had a strong, sometimes demanding, personality

Howard had simply meant that he didn't want me to become subservient to people like George Foerstner. He wanted me to always remain my own man. He wanted me to be 100 percent confident in making my own decisions.

101

Howard Hall was a great man, a great mentor, a great friend. If you ever have the opportunity to become close to such a man, hang on to it. Even after death, the principles he taught me are right up there with my mother's.

Chapter 32

The First Bank

Since I had founded, operated and sold Swisher Farm Supply for a profit, I knew that was the way to go. Own the business if you want to make money. Somebody told me that along the way, and getting into a partnership with John Hamilton and Forbes Olberg at Merchant's National Bank to form our own JEFCO Corp. solidified that notion.

I had this craving to own a bank. I had observed how that, when you go to bed at night, the clock keeps ticking away and the bank earns interest. If you own the bank, it's your interest that's growing.

Now, I couldn't buy just any bank. It had to be small enough that I could afford it. It had to be somewhat close to Cedar Rapids so I could visit regularly. It had to be for sale, or at least have a manager and a board of directors that were open to being bought.

The Farmers Savings Bank in Martelle fit the bill.

In 1960 I approached Guy Martin, the bank's manager and cashier, met with the board of directors and looked at the bank's balance sheets. Farmers Savings Bank was a little more than 40 years old (chartered in 1917) and had survived after the big stock market crash in 1929 that led to the closure of so many banks and, eventually, The Great Depression. The bank was turning a profit of less than $10,000 a year, which went to stockholders, the undivided profits and its capital fund, but I didn't care. I just wanted a bank.

If I remember right, the Martelle bank had assets of about $800,000 at the time. When you buy a bank, though, you don't buy out the assets. That money belongs to the depositors. What you pay for is the capital (the charter, the building, the fixtures, etc.) and the undivided profits. "Undivided profits" is the accounting balance sheet of the bank's earnings that didn't get distributed to the stockholders plus an accounting of the loan losses if you need to write them off. It can get rather complicated.

The Farmers Savings Bank in Martelle, the first bank purchased by Ernie Buresh, as it looks today.

In this case, I paid about $75,000 to become the majority stockholder, to become the owner of the Farmers Savings Bank in Martelle. I was able to borrow that entire amount from Merchant's National Bank by working with S.E. Coquillette, the president and a close friend of Howard Hall's.

To secure such a large loan, I had my older brother, Les, co-sign the papers. He owned the International Harvester dealership in Mount Vernon so that served as collateral. Les became president of our bank.

The first order of business, of course, is to elect a board of directors and get management in place. We kept the board intact, which I'd promised during the negotiations. And Guy Martin stayed on to manage the bank, although he was ready to retire, which is why everyone had agreed to sell the bank.

I certainly wasn't going to run the bank. I didn't know the first thing about it and I was working in the trust department at Merchants National Bank. So I nosed around and checked the Iowa Bankers newsletter for potential leads. That's when we hired a young man by the name of Guy Sleep.

He turned out to be the most knowledgeable, able banker I've ever met. He had incredible loan analyzing ability, incredible knowledge in the operations of a bank and, most of all, an incredible personality. The people you hire make all the difference in the world in your own success.

Chapter 33

The First Board

When Al Morrisey, an insurance man in Mount Vernon, agreed to take an early open seat on our Board of Directors at Farmers Saving Bank in Martelle, we knew we were going to be in good hands. I don't know of a finer individual than Al. Since this was our early days in banking, we really needed somebody of his caliber, which certainly added a lot to the bank's reputation.

Al was a good friend to my brother, Les, who had the Mount Vernon International Harvester dealership. Since Les was going to be president of the bank, Al agreed to purchase some of our available stock to be on the board.

Al Morrisey, a Mount Vernon insurance agent, was on Ernie Buresh's first bank board.

Al was a perfect fit, having been in business for years and knowing a lot of people in the area. But he was a good fit, too, because he was not only a man of integrity, he was an astute businessman who could

106

read other people like few men I've ever known.

This was so important, especially when getting started, because the main role of a bank's board is to examine and approve loans. Al's common sense and local knowledge were big reasons we had a high success rate in our loan department. He knew I never wanted to assume that any of our loans would be bad. Al stayed with us the rest of his life.

An example of Al's integrity came up when he had the opportunity to buy a farm on the southeast corner of Highway 1 and Highway 30 in Mount Vernon It's now developed into businesses that include Hardees and Dairy Queen. Al asked Les and me if we wanted to be a part of it. We knew it was a good deal. In my opinion it was a no-brainer. But Al was such a good guy we didn't want to dilute his interest in that investment.

Al's local connections also brought about the election of Arland Christ-Janer, the president at Cornell College in Mount Vernon, to our board. He was on our board until 1967 when he left Cornell to become president at Boston University. Al was on the board of trustees at Cornell which led to me becoming a lifetime trustee at Cornell.

Yes, if it wasn't for my brother, I wouldn't have had the good fortune to meet somebody like Al. If it wasn't for Al, I might not have met Arland, the first college president I could call my friend. I learned a lot from both men, the most valuable being the importance of building strong relationships. Al built his business that way, Arland helped Cornell grow that way, so it was only natural that we'd apply the same ideals to banking.

Chapter 34

Guy Sleep

Hiring Guy Sleep from out in the boondocks of southwest Iowa, from Bedford, to manage Farmers Savings Bank in Martelle was not a no-brainer. He sounded good on paper, but he was younger than me and I was only 33. How much could someone that young really know about banking?

Besides, when the bank's board of directors, Les and I examined his application, we had second thoughts. He didn't look very good from the picture he sent. When he arrived for an interview, he was driving a beat-up old car. And then he was so young, maybe too young. But, if he worked out, that possibly could be a good thing, we thought, because he might stick around for a while.

Guy Sleep, who was hired by Ernie to manage his first bank, as he looked in 1973.

Anyway, we took a chance and hired Guy Sleep. I still have the letter (July 18, 1960) when he accepted the job for $7,500 a year. After all, we weren't a huge metropolitan bank – we were a small bank in a small town in rural Iowa that catered to the farm population.

Immediately, as we began remodeling the bank and doing some promotions, it became apparent that hiring Guy Sleep was the best move we could have made. He had an amazing sense of reality, of being fiscally responsible. Yet, he wanted to spruce up the building so it would operate more efficiently and be attractive to new depositors.

That was my main priority in buying the bank, to figure out a way to make it grow.

Guy had it all figured out.

The secret, of course, is to treat your customers as you want to be treated. We didn't hand out free toasters or blankets to get people in the door. We weren't interest cutters for the sake of beating the competition.

No. Our emphasis was on the individual, on each person who came into Farmers Savings Bank. We did what we could for each of them to operate their businesses, their farms. We built relationships. Pretty soon they wouldn't do anything financially without talking to us first, without talking to Guy. If they couldn't afford to pay a loan back, we explained exactly why we couldn't give them the money at this time. We were nice about it. They understood. Maybe we'd be able to help them with something else down the road.

You know, banking is intriguing when you take a look at it. It's not about making money for the bank. It's about working every day for your customers. If they don't succeed, you don't succeed. A lot of banks have lost track of that.

I've got to thank Guy Sleep. He's an example of how important relationships are. We hired Guy out of the blue and put him in charge of a bank. In return, he worked for us the rest of his career.

In fact, I genuinely felt I worked for Guy more than having him work for us. We never made a banking decision without talking it over with Guy. He taught me everything I know about owning a bank. Everything.

Chapter 35

On to Anamosa

As business at Farmers Savings Bank in Martelle picked up, we realized that larger growth could only come by expanding our coverage area. Les, Guy Sleep and I decided that moving the bank's charter to Anamosa would do the trick.

When I talked to Joanne's father, George Paulsen, the Onslow banker, he suggested that the purchase of the Citizens Savings Bank in Anamosa might be a good solution. George had a strong working relationship with that bank.

Citizens Savings Bank had been in Anamosa about 60 years. It had survived the Depression as the only bank left in town. It had been in the Wegman family for years.

If we could make a deal, they'd sell. If we couldn't, they wouldn't. It was as simple as that.

In 1963, the pieces all came together. We had negotiated with Leonard Wegman and took over a majority interest. The bank had assets of about $6 million, or eight times the assets of the Martelle bank when we'd assumed ownership there. That meant a bigger loan for us, which we secured through Merchants National Bank in Cedar Rapids. It also meant more potential.

In fact, I don't believe in hiring consultants because it's the biggest waste of money there is, but I made an exception here. We hired Frank N. Magid and Associates of Marion to survey people in Anamosa to find out about their banking needs and what they lacked. That helped us determine what to offer to attract new customers.

While my brother remained president of the Martelle bank and continued to operate his implement dealership in Mount Vernon, I became president in Anamosa and continued my job at Merchants National Bank. Guy Sleep began spending more time in Anamosa as our right-hand man.

While we'd taken a little look into the history of the Anamosa bank, that wasn't our main concern. We didn't care so much about what had happened before as we cared about working to make it better in the future.

By now I was close to Howard Hall. I don't remember talking to him a lot about this personal decision, but he neither encouraged it or discouraged it. He had faith in me, I guess. And with this purchase I figured, when you're in it this deep, you're in it for good.

Anamosa provided us with higher assets, more depositors and more borrowers, which obviously is how you make money in the banking business, but it's also the riskiest part. We got along fine, but as president I thought it was time I became more hands-on rather than working at another bank, even though it was going to be a completely new experience. Guy Sleep would be invaluable in helping with the transition.

When we'd bought the Martelle bank the people at Merchants National Bank had all known I was eventually going to leave. I worked full time there until my last day and then it was on to Anamosa full time.

Joanne and the girls – Wendy was 11 and Sandy, 8 1/2 – were fine with moving to Anamosa in 1963. They knew it was what I needed to do. And all of us liked the community better and better the more time we spent there.

Joanne and I found a beautiful two-story stone house on North Ford Street in Anamosa. It had been built with the last stone taken from the Reformatory Quarry before it closed. We would go from three bedrooms and two bathrooms in Swisher to three bedrooms and three bathrooms in Anamosa. But the house was better planned and it was larger; a lot nicer house than we left behind.

The home on North Ford in Anamosa as it looks today became home to the Buresh family in 1963.

Some people might have been sad to leave behind a house they had put so much sweat equity into, but that wasn't a concern at all since we were able to sell the Swisher house for $22,000, the exact same price they wanted for the house in Anamosa.

I mean, how fortunate can you be? We bought a nicer house without a mortgage – in fact, I've never made a home mortgage payment in my life. I've borrowed a lot of money, but I've never borrowed it for a house.

We moved with the help of friends and their pickups. And when we needed more furniture for the larger house we found used furniture that worked just fine. We rarely bought anything new.

That's the thing. Invest in your future, not in the present. You don't need new possessions to be happy. I learned that growing up poor and Joanne was with me.

Sure, you sometimes wonder if you're making the right decisions. But I'm like my mother. If things change, you just keep going. Don't waste time worrying about it.

After they'd settled in Anamosa, a swimming pool and tennis court (left) shown in 1986, provided fun and recreation for the Buresh family behind the "Tennis Shack" across Ford Street from their stone home.

Along with the household and family move to Anamosa, I set up my office at the Citizens Savings Bank on the north side of Main Street. This was in the heart of the Anamosa business district. I was 38 years old, had been a researcher, a salesman, a feed business owner, a house builder, a trust officer in a bank, a husband and a father. Now we were on to an entirely new chapter.

ERNIE BURESH

A Future to Bank On

Chapter 36

Bridge is in the Cards

The first thing Joanne and I learned about Anamosa was that it's a bridge playing town. We'd been in a pinochle card club in Swisher. We were playing Five Hundred once a month after a dinner with a group of my Army buddies and their wives, a tradition that would carry on for more than 50 years. Cards came second nature. But bridge was an entirely new game for more reasons than one.

I was settling into my office at the Citizens Savings Bank and learning the nuances of being a bank president from Guy Sleep. Joanne and our daughters, Wendy and Sandy, were making friends and starting classes at their new school. When you're new to a community, you look for ways to socialize.

After we heard that bridge was the game to play in Anamosa, we thought it would be fun to join a bridge club. This was the 1960s, after all, when bridge was very popular all around the country. We had never played bridge until then, but I'd grown up with a deck of cards in my hand. It was a cheap form of entertainment when you're poor and my mother loved to teach me games, although we usually played pinochle.

When a lot of business people – especially men – think about making important social connections in the business community, they often think of golf as the activity most likely to succeed. I tried golf earlier but gave it up. I was no good at it. I don't have the patience. I didn't have the time because it would take hours.

I always believed – and Howard Hall was with me on this – that any business relationship in golf developed either before you started to play, as you got ready to hit the ball on the first tee, or after the round was over. During the game itself, you concentrated on your play.

Howard Hall once told me while we watched a group of men tee off after we'd eaten lunch, that if they had time to play golf in the middle of the day, they either didn't have any business or they weren't taking care of what they had.

Bridge, on the other hand, took place in the evenings, at least in those days in Anamosa. It took half as long as a round of golf. You visited other people in their homes and hosted them in yours. It was an opportunity to show your hospitality. And even though you'd concentrate on the game, you had plenty of time to visit when the cards were being shuffled and dealt because you were sitting around a table, not riding a golf cart or walking in the opposite direction of the people you wanted to get to know.

I remember one time soon after we'd moved to Anamosa that I was invited to substitute for a men's bridge club. Of course, you played for money. Not a lot, but it made the game more interesting. I know I lost, probably not any more than a dollar. But men at that game never forgot what I said at the end of the night and it has followed me throughout my bridge career.

After settling up with the wagers, I told the men, "Don't call me, I'll call you." Sure, I wanted to win. Everybody wants to win. But, in cards, you need to learn it's just a game.

120

Joanne and I have been playing bridge for 50 years. She still gets back to Anamosa to play bridge with her regular group. Since we moved to Cedar Rapids 25 years ago I frequently join a group at the Cedar Rapids Country Club for the same reason I've always played cards – to build and maintain relationships.

Bridge is a great game. You play with a partner. It's a lot better than watching TV. It sure is good for the mind.

Now I've reached a stage in bridge where it's much more enjoyable for me to play with partners that use conventions.

That's what makes bridge such a good game for anyone. You can easily learn the basics, that spades and hearts are the major suits, that you need to bid only what you can take in tricks and that one or two bad hands don't have to ruin your night. But, when you advance to using conventions – the signals partners can give each other to indicate the strengths and weaknesses of their hand – it becomes a much more challenging and rewarding game. Now you've got strategy and you've really got to think.

A while back I tried playing bridge on a computer but it's not the same. You don't have the personal interaction. I'm not alone. I had to laugh when I heard that two people I greatly admire – Bill Gates, the co-founder of Microsoft, and Warren Buffet, the billionaire investor – want to convince more people to learn how to play bridge. I would love to get into a game with them some day. Their interest in bridge just confirms I was on the right track all along.

Chapter 37

Observations: Ernie's Desk

A businessman's desk becomes his home away from home. In Ernie Buresh's case, since he has worked at a desk for more than 60 years, it is his u-shaped work area in the basement of Hilltop, his Cedar Rapids home.

Tucked away down a semi-circular stairway at the end of a long hallway lined with pictures of a life well lived, Ernie's desk is cluttered with papers, mementos and nine coffee cups all filled with pens and pencils.

"That's a habit you fall into," Ernie laughs. "You have a pen, you think it's running out of ink, so you take another one."

Pens are a big part of banking, Ernie's business life for 52 years. They advertise banks. They advertise customers' businesses. They're ready to be taken in hand to jot down random notes, phone numbers, tax figures, personal correspondence. You don't want to run out of ink.

As Ernie and I chat, my pen runs dry. "Don't worry about it," Ernie says. "I've got plenty." And he plucks one out of a coffee cup and hands it to me.

Seated on a four-legged wooden chair, Ernie has everything he needs at his fingertips – a couple of staplers, trays with paper clips, a metal spike to plop papers onto so they don't blow away, a dispenser that holds two rolls of cellophane tape.

On the main desk sits Ernie's printing calculator attached by red rubber bands to a clear plastic stand with extra rolls of adding machine paper nearby. His phone is there, too, with speaker phone capability. To his right, hanging from a wire, are strips cut from file folders with names and phone numbers jotted down as he needed them, not in any other particular order. Behind him rests the tan IBM electric typewriter that's been with him for maybe 40 years. To his left, a rolling file cabinet with a top drawer divided like that of a cash register holds important reference papers.

"I had a great day," Ernie says on this February morning. He'd been plugging tax numbers into his calculator – a recent replacement for a reliable old one – and after rechecking the numbers, his calculations had come out right to the penny.

The typewriter – Ernie types out checks and occasional correspondence – works perfectly although it has been repaired a time or two. "It's hard to get it worked on any more," Ernie says. "I know the last time I had it fixed, the bill was more than I originally paid for it."

These two items – the calculator and the typewriter – are as trusty and steadfast as Ernie's best friends. He has befriended people from all walks of life and kept them close for decades. As he talks, I hear names I've never heard and names as famous as any in Iowa. With Ernie, that's just the way it is when it comes to friends. "These people deserve recognition for how they have helped me, because, with them, you know I'm not the only one," he says from behind his strong and sturdy desk.

The lights of a computer connected to the internet blink in the distance on another desk that Ernie rarely visits. Even though he likes to make payments by phone and carries an "antique" flip-open cell phone, Ernie doesn't need a computer himself. This one, and one not hooked up on another desk, were for Jean Hoppenrath, his personal secretary for more than 40 years from his early days at City National Bank until she retired three or four years ago.

Ernie Buresh reads an early draft of this book at his desk in the lower level of Hilltop.

Ernie's work area resides off to the side of a spacious room that includes two more desks and some heavy duty folding tables piled with papers and other mementos. On the wall above the computer hangs a large black-and-white sketch of Hilltop surrounded by six smaller drawings of Anamosa landmarks including the stone barn, the stone water tower and the stone general store. The other walls are covered with prints of Grant Wood paintings around Stone City, pictures of people Ernie has known – among them University of Iowa presidents, former University of Iowa football coach Hayden Fry, and politicians Bob Ray, Ted Kennedy and Dan Quayle – and his diploma from Iowa State University as well as the composite picture of his graduating class from the University of Iowa Law School.

"I did feel honored to be on a first-name basis with all of the presidents of the university since the year I graduated law school," Ernie says.

While one of the pen-filled coffee cups on his desk advertises the law school, another reads Dartmouth, a gift from former U of I President James O. Freedman who left Iowa for the Ivy League.

"A major concern I have now is downsizing," Ernie says. "This is a Czech trait. Never throw anything away." He smiles. "I keep thinking I'm going to clean this all up and have a nice clean desk. I never get it done."

Sure, there's stuff he won't use – thumb tacks and a couple of old computer floppy discs – and things he'd forgotten were there – a box with a three-cent stamp and a card designating him Anamosa's Chamber of Commerce member for November, 1989.

But there are so many things here Ernie couldn't live without. Shelves on the wall to his right hold sandbox toys and dozens of other trinkets given to him through the years by loyal customers. There's a bust of President Abraham Lincoln simply because Ernie respects him as a great man. Since Ernie's a bridge player, the book "Goren Settles the Bridge Arguments" rests on a corner of his desk. Off to one side sits an empty glass candy jar from St. Luke's Hospital in Cedar Rapids.

Oh yes, Ernie still uses the candy jar. He laughs. "I have peppermints in there when I can afford to buy them."

On a tall bookshelf stands a pair of intricate wooden carriage clocks that had belonged to his grandmother, Barbara Stanek.

On the board behind him are pictures of former University of Iowa basketball coaches – a color photo of Joanne and Ernie with Tom Davis and a fading color picture clipped from a newspaper of Lute Olson, whose fingers are adorned with championship rings from the University of Arizona where he coached after Iowa.

University of Iowa men's basketball coach Lute Olson also grew up poor.

"Joanne and I were close friends with Lute and his (late) wife Bobbi," Ernie says. "We'd get into discussions about who grew up poorer. I finally relented that Lute had been poorer than I was. That's really something because he is really successful."

Still in a box is a toy truck from Heartland Express, the company founded by Russ Gerdin who died in 2011. "What to do with it, I don't know," Ernie says. "I want to keep it. Russ was my best friend."

On Ernie's desk, he'll turn on the radio for a basketball game when it's not on TV and, if he works on a Sunday morning, to listen to polka music. He often gazes at the picture of his wife, Joanne, and smaller black and white photos of his daughters, Wendy and Sandy, when they were quite young. Pigeon-holed here and there are Father's Day cards and a small gold medallion imprinted with a prayer from television evangelist The Rev. Dr. Robert Schuller whom Sandy adored and got to meet once.

When Ernie Buresh works – "I don't see how some people who retire get all of their stuff done." – he surrounds himself with important pieces of his life – his principles, his friends and his family. That is how you come to realize your dreams.

Dave Rasdal

Chapter 38

Into the Metro Area

My feet were barely wet in Anamosa when Howard Hall began talking about selling his interest in City National Bank, which he had founded. The Cedar Rapids entrepreneur was nearing 70 years old and had been in business a long time. While he was still very active, I think he was ready to slow down a little.

Howard had enlisted my help with City National Bank in the late 1950s, soon after I'd joined the trust department at Merchants National Bank. Together, we'd talk about ideas to improve not only the bottom line of City National, but to improve its standing in the community. As a result of that success, I bought some stock in City National to show my faith in its future.

Citizens Savings Bank in Anamosa as it looks today with three drive-up windows to the left.

Of course, I was very busy in Anamosa then, too. We built a new bank and opened it in 1965 with the first drive-up window in Jones County. In fact, we had two drive-up windows. The Citizens Savings Bank building at Main Street and Cleveland Street used Stone City stone and the dark paneling popular at the time. Our assets topped $9 million that year.

A brochure introduced Citizens Savings Bank customers to the new bank with a drive-up window in 1965.

Soon, Howard urged me to put together a deal to acquire a majority interest in his bank which had about one-and-a-half times the assets of Citizens Savings Bank. I think it was his way of rewarding me for helping him turn City National around. So he made some of his stock available and he urged other people on the board to do the same. His board at that time included a lot of influential people in the Cedar Rapids and Marion communities. Buying the bank was a no-brainer because Howard still planned to stay involved.

City National became my third bank and I was president there, just as I was president in Anamosa.

But Guy Sleep, who had been instrumental in our success at the Martelle bank and then at Anamosa, even though I was officially president, moved on to perform his magic at City National.

People who aren't in the banking business need to understand this is only a title. A president is just somebody who's necessary. Actually, a bank president runs everything through the bank's board. The president just keeps the motor running.

Every loan – it doesn't matter how little or how much – needs the board's approval. When a loan is presented to the board, whether by a loan officer or the president, the board's job is to look at the risk factors, to determine if making the loan is a wise decision.

Of course, the larger the loan, the more scrutiny it faces. If we're talking about a $1,000 loan, it has probably gone through approval and simply appears on a list for the board to approve. But, that doesn't mean it might not have some risk, too.

A board member could look at the list and recognize a name. "I know that deadbeat," he might say. But, by then it's too late.

One thing I learned early is that you can't avoid an occasional deadbeat, someone who isn't very reliable about paying back their loan. But you've also got to be wary of offending a deadbeat because deadbeats have friends. Not only do those friends repeat whatever a deadbeat might tell them, but maybe they'll come in for a loan some day, too, and that friend will become a great customer.

Chapter 39

Aid to the Hospital

A year or so after we moved to Anamosa, the Sisters of Mercy made it known that they could no longer afford to keep the hospital open. It was an old stone building, tucked beyond a hill just east of the Anamosa State Reformatory. It needed a lot of repairs and the Sisters just didn't have the money.

People in Anamosa were saddened by the news. After all, the Sisters of Mercy first opened a hospital in town in 1894. A hospital is vital to a community. I said the bank would do what it could to help keep the hospital operating.

The Sisters, with most of their efforts concentrated in Cedar Rapids, had plenty of other worthwhile projects. Our main order of business was to convince them to stay and the best way to do that was to promise – at least say we'd try – to raise enough money to build a new hospital.

Well, the community fundraising succeeded. We raised money from not only Anamosa, but also all around Jones County, and we even got a substantial contribution from a woman in New York City who had ties to Anamosa.

The old hospital was torn down and the new hospital was built in its place. That hospital served the community of Anamosa for several decades until a few years ago when the new Jones County Regional Medical Center at the east edge of town opened.

I've always believed a community needs a hospital, so that's why the bank made a substantial contribution to the fundraiser in the 1960s. It's also why I worked on the campaign and was able to make a small contribution on my own. When the hospital had outgrown that building and its board decided a new, larger hospital was needed, I supported that, too. Joanne and I were able to make another contribution to that hospital building.

Ernie Buresh, a strong supporter of a hospital in Anamosa since the 1960s, stands outside the main entrance to the Jones County Regional Medical Center at Anamosa.

The new hospital is wonderful, but I feel a little embarrassed to walk through the main entrance. Above it the sign reads "Joanne and Ernie Buresh Building." They insisted on naming the building after Joanne and me. I thought it was all right because Joanne was born in the old hospital, but I've never given money to something to have my name put on it.

I'm just a big believer in philanthropy. I know some people like to pile it up, to assemble as much wealth as they can. That's okay. But along the way you ought to recognize that you've had good fortune and support good causes that you believe in. This goes right back to my mother, that when you give of yourself it comes back to you over and over and over.

I'll tell you what means as much to me as anything. I still have some of the old stained glass windows from that old hospital building. I grabbed them out of a Dumpster before they got broken. One of the windows hangs in a west-facing window on the porch of our home in Cedar Rapids. The evening light really brings it to life.

Chapter 40

Sandy's Surgeries

As Sandy, our youngest daughter, grew a little older, it soon became evident that her heart would need some special attention. She was potty trained at two and she could talk, although I often had trouble understanding what she said. Joanne and Sandy's older sister, Wendy, were my interpreters. They seemed to catch every word. But, no matter how hard Sandy tried, she still had trouble walking very far and she would tire easily.

We'd been taking her to Children's Memorial Hospital in Chicago for regular checkups every six months. That's when we'd ride the train from Marion to Chicago and back. When doctors told us she'd need surgery, they wanted to wait until she was 30 pounds. They wanted to make sure she'd be strong enough to survive it.

Well, by the time Sandy was five she only weighed 29 pounds. She was always small for her age. The doctors said that would be good enough and scheduled her for surgery.

Sandy had a ventricular septal defect in her heart, which meant there was a hole between the left and right ventricles. The doctors had to split her breastbone, hook her up to a heart bypass machine, put a patch in her little heart and take her off the bypass machine and hope her heart started up again.

133

Let me just say it was hard every time Sandy had surgery. But that first time I'm not sure I was prepared. What parent can be? When I saw her hooked up to all the equipment, the drainage tubes, the tubes from her heart, the tube so she could breathe, it was very traumatic. She was such a tiny thing. It was the look on her face that really gets to you. She was so brave. But I had to leave the room.

Recovery took a couple of weeks in Chicago. Joanne and I slept in Sandy's room a couple of nights. Then I had to get back home to work at the bank and to take care of Wendy. Joanne's parents also went to Chicago and were with her for support. I don't know that Joanne ever left Sandy's room.

Doctors had also discovered that Sandy had a paralyzed palate. It's not unusual that a child born with a defect will have more than one. That's why I had trouble understanding what she was saying. She could speak but it didn't come out like she wanted it to. Her palate was developed, it just didn't move.

Wendy and Sandy Buresh wear matching Annie Oakley outfits in 1958.

So, when Sandy was seven, she had both her tonsils and her adenoids removed in preparation for palate surgery. We took her to University Hospitals in Iowa City where doctors sewed her palate to the back of her throat so she had some muscle control over it. The result was that she couldn't

134

breathe through her nose, that she lost her sense of smell and some of her sense of taste. But it did improve her speech.

And then, when Sandy was ten, doctors in Chicago said they needed to operate on her heart again. It seemed that there was a problem with her aorta, that it had been nicked during the first surgery. The patch they'd used then had holes in it so it wouldn't restrict the growth of her heart too much. They had to put new patches on her heart to make it more secure. She had three patches on her heart for the rest of her life.

After the second heart surgery, Sandy had to stay in the hospital longer than expected because she would have a fever every night. The doctors also said they were amazed she'd survived the palate surgery, since they didn't know we were having that done. Sandy was a proud little girl. She was so brave. We were so happy to have her back home again.

Sandy Buresh (left) receives a hug from Nan Wood Graham, sister of famous artist Grant Wood, during a 1970s visit to the Grant Wood Art Festival in Stone City.

Chapter 41

Grant Wood Country and Nan

Once you live in Jones County, it's in your heart forever. If you don't believe me, just look at Grant Wood. He was born there and left when he was a child, yet so many of the paintings he created as an adult bring you back to Jones County. He had his art colony in Stone City in the 1930s.

When people in Anamosa talked about having a festival to honor Grant Wood we supported it one-hundred percent. Before it started in the 1970s, we were able to work with George Nissen, the Cedar Rapids man who developed and promoted the trampoline, since he owned the old barn in Stone City. He opened up that barn for the festival which really gave it the old-time flavor.

Citizens Savings Bank also did its part, sponsoring and putting together a replica of one of the old art wagons like Grant Wood had used in his Stone City art colony in the 1930s. When it came festival time in June, I was glad to do whatever I could for the cause, whatever they needed me to do, directing traffic, parking cars, taking tickets. You need a lot of people to put on an event like that so we had our whole bank crew volunteer.

Not everything worked out, though. We once had Sammy Kaye, the legendary band leader, come to perform at the festival and it wasn't a hit. I probably should have had somebody from Iowa play, somebody like my good friend Leonard Reyman who grew up around Swisher and had a dance band for decades.

One thing I remember about Sammy Kaye's appearance was that it was a hot day. During a break, we talked and he said something about needing a drink. Well, no alcohol was served at the festival and I don't drink, but I had some stuff for entertaining at the house. I took Sammy Kaye to our house in Anamosa, fixed him a drink, I don't know what, and he went back to finish the day.

A steel beam is inserted into the floor between the main level and upper floor during remodeling of the General Store in Stone City in 1970.

We became such firm believers in preserving Stone City even before the art festival, so in 1970, when the General Store and the Blacksmith Shop came up for sale, Joanne and I bought them.

We completely remodeled the General Store, including having a steel beam inserted beneath the upper floor to make sure it was stable. We also had two fireplaces and a bar installed during the remodeling and were able to use it for some gatherings of the University of Iowa football team coaches.

The Blacksmith shop was remodeled, too, so it could be used for the Grant Wood Art Festival. It became a popular attraction for the crowds that showed up.

Later, Joanne and I donated both buildings to worthwhile causes – the General Store to the University of Iowa Foundation which sold it, and the Blacksmith Shop to the Stone City Foundation which still owns it.

Joanne and Ernie Buresh pose for a picture in front of the Blacksmith Shop in Stone City after they had purchased the shop and had it fixed up for the Grant Wood Art Festival.

The highlight for us from the first year of the Grant Wood Art Festival was that Grant Wood's sister, Nan Wood Graham, came for a visit. She needed a place to stay, so we opened up our home to her. What a wonderful, sweet lady. That was the start of a fantastic relationship until Nan died in 1990. She was 91.

Whenever Nan came to the festival and needed a place to stay, she'd stay with us. We visited her several times in California, too, when she lived in Riverside. The first time we went out with the whole family, she had a red carpet unrolled in front of her house for Wendy and Sandy, Joanne and me. We also visited her for her 90th birthday party when she lived in a care center in Menlo Park, not far from Stanford University.

Nan Wood Graham (left), sister of famous artist Grant Wood, poses with Joanne and Ernie Buresh in the 1970s during a visit to Anamosa and the Grant Wood Art Festival in Stone City.

Our relationship grew strong because we'd write letters back and forth, but also because Nan would have her confidant send me her financial dealings to make sure nobody was ripping her off.

If you don't know, Nan was the model for the woman in her brother's American Gothic painting. She spent her life protecting his reputation and legacy. She was able to do that because she received royalties for the use of his paintings.

After Nan died I was surprised that she had our family in her will. She left daughter Sandy something like $10,000 which we then donated to the National Czech & Slovak Museum & Library for the carillon music. And she left Joanne and me a portion of the royalties from American Gothic. Now, more than 20 years later, we still get a check every three months for $200 or $300. It's pretty amazing to have a connection to such a famous painting.

Chapter 42

A Million Dollars in Debt

In my mind, three banks weren't enough. It boils down to what presents an opportunity to improve what you already have. I knew that buying these little banks wasn't going to set the world on fire, but they were interesting challenges.

You like to have more challenges. You want to see how changes you'd make would improve the status and strengths of a bank. Basically, you want to see what you can accomplish.

So, in the ensuing years I bought banks in Springville (The Exchange State Bank), Tipton (First National Bank) and Onslow (Onslow Savings Bank), where Joanne's dad, George Paulsen, continued to work. We also built the new Citizens Savings Bank building in Anamosa in 1965 which had the first drive-up window in town.

At one time I was a million dollars in debt. I never owed money for a mortgage on a house, but expanding your businesses is a different matter even though everybody doesn't necessarily see it that way.

I have to laugh about the day Joanne and I were visiting her folks in Onslow and her dad came into the house with a copy of the Des Moines Register under his arm. It had a story that Bankers Trust in Des Moines had been sold. George showed me the headline and said, "There's one you missed."

Anyway, it's hard to figure out the exact peak of debt, but I know it topped seven figures. As long as the banks were profitable, I was comfortable. You could tell each month if the banks were making money.

The Exchange State Bank in Springville today with a covered drive-up window to the right.

When it came to looking at the figures, I had one-hundred-percent confidence in Guy Sleep. He's the one who kept the books and knew exactly what was going on. I had two-hundred-percent faith in his abilities to analyze every aspect of every purchase.

Of course, I didn't want to be in debt any longer than necessary. You had to borrow the money from larger banks and you paid interest, just like anybody who borrowed from our banks for their businesses. The payback time frame depended on the size of the loan, but I know that every loan we took out to buy a bank, we paid back early. There was no penalty for that. In fact, it helps the bottom line. Early payback is a no-brainer.

During this time I met other people who owned banks so I was able to observe and learn from them.

One of those people was Mel Happel, a Van Horne banker who decided to acquire Farmers Savings Bank in Victor. I agreed to serve on his board of directors for a few years because I thought it would help both of us out. Victor was far enough away there wasn't any conflict of interest with our banks. And, let me tell you, Mel had a great board – it was always a pleasure to attend their meetings.

In 2000 I decided to build a bank on the Shueyville farm because housing in that area was expanding by leaps and bounds and there wasn't a bank in the area on the east side of I-380. We were able to use the Springville charter to open a branch office of the Exchange State Bank in Shueyville.

It was a great challenge to design the building – I studied other plans and learned from them – and a pleasure to watch Paul Nielsen build it. When it was done, there wasn't anything we'd change.

By then, we'd grown large enough we didn't need to buy or open any more banks. Sometimes you can get too big. You need to know when you're right where you want to be and this was it.

Chapter 43

A Nickel is a Nickel

When I see an empty beverage can along the side of the road I have this unquenchable desire to stop and pick it up. When you see a can thrown away in a parking lot, you wonder who does it. You wonder why.

I don't understand it for two reasons. One is financial. The other is the lack of respect for the environment. I wouldn't think of throwing a can out.

No. I'll take it home and get rid of it. A nickel is a nickel. A dollar is a dollar. Anything like this you save is saved after taxes. It's a double saving.

Look at the cost of paper. A box of paper might cost $25. That's clean paper on both sides. But I reuse paper. In the fax machine I can put it in dirty side up and use the clean side. I can do it with the copy machine, too.

These aren't big things, but it also doesn't take a lot of effort to do them.

I know people will read this and say, I'm not going to do that with one can or for one sheet of paper. A lot of times people don't admit to doing things that are wasteful to save embarrassment. Just like they don't admit to throwing an empty can out the window or leaving it in a parking lot.

Neatness is heavenly. Return your cans regularly.

When we bought the Springville bank, I was amazed to find the basement full of empty bottles. I think at

144

the time you could get two cents per bottle. We took them back and got more than $10. Do you know how many bottles that is?

You know, ten bucks is ten bucks.

Chapter 44

A Loan for a Friend

If you haven't done it, you might think that making a loan to a friend could be troublesome. It never bothered me. From my standpoint, it's always a business transaction with certain parameters. You loan the money at the going interest rate and the borrower pays it back within the promised time frame.

If anything bothered me about making loans, it was when someone came in with a cosigner. I did everything I could to discourage cosigned loans. The problem is that cosigners think all they're doing is making it possible for a friend or relative to borrow money. What they're really doing is promising to pay back the money if the borrower doesn't. They're on the hook. It doesn't happen very often that a cosigner has to pay, but it happens more often than you think.

Sometimes, I admit, you can get caught up in your own rules and make a mistake.

One of those mistakes was with Pete Gombert, a very successful businessman today in the Anamosa area who developed the lake and housing development near Highway 151 and Highway 1. Early in my banking career, Pete came into the Anamosa bank to borrow $1,000. I don't even remember why he wanted the money. His grandmother was going to cosign and I turned him down.

In Pete's case, I missed seeing that he was a hard worker. I didn't have enough information. The problem is that people will come in and you've never had any contact with them before. Sometimes you misjudge.

I'm fortunate in Pete's case. He became successful in a variety of businesses. He still treats me as a friend even though I turned him down for a loan.

I don't recall anyone ever asking for special favors just because we were friends. They might joke about it, but then you joke back. You'd tell them, always buy green bananas because they'll last longer. Or, we have two interest rates – high and higher. Which one do you want?

When you look at a borrower, you look at two things. Why does he need the money or why does he think he needs the money? What's his commitment to not only get the money, but to pay it back? The most important thing for the banker is to stand back, to look at the situation, to be fair.

When I had surgery recently, my surgeon was a former loan customer. I told him, now don't look at this as an opportunity to get even for the interest rate I had to charge you. He laughed. He told me I was always fair.

As a banker, there are no words sweeter than that. Your goal is to always be fair. When the customer sees it that way you know you've done your job.

Chapter 45

Farm Crisis of the '80s

If people in Eastern Iowa remember anything about what was called the farm crisis of 30 years ago, they remember that a farmer in financial trouble walked into Hills Bank & Trust in Hills and killed his banker, John Hughes.

I was just shocked when I heard about it, that's what I remember. I don't think it mattered that it was a banker. John was a good friend.

I met John Hughes through a bank function a few years before he was shot. We talked about this and that and learned that we both enjoyed playing bridge. Pretty soon we had a monthly bridge game going. One month he'd get three other people – directors or employees from his bank or other friends – together and come up to Anamosa to play against me and three friends. Then, the next month, we'd meet in Iowa City because that's where he lived.

When we played bridge it was a social occasion. If we talked bank business, that was rare. Playing cards was fun and took our minds off work. We kept score, I know, but we didn't play for any money. John was a good player and a great guy. He was like any banker in those days – he didn't like the high, double-digit inflation rates any more than the people who wanted loans. He tried to work with them. He didn't deserve to die.

The financial crisis of the early 1980s was tough on all businesses that needed to borrow money. High interest rates meant prices went up and that just contributed to inflation.

I thoroughly enjoyed visiting with farmers. They're ordinary people, just like the rest of us, trying to make a living. I really admire their willingness to do the hard work a farmer is required to do. When you're a farmer, there are all sorts of risks – the weather, prices in the future, managing your own finances. You want to get ahead and often that means you want to grow bigger, add more land.

This is where the difference between needs and wants enters the picture. In Anamosa at this time we tried to discourage farmers from buying any more land, from getting new equipment, from spending money they absolutely didn't need to spend. These were things they wanted. We encouraged them to just take care of what they had. If they needed to borrow money for feeder livestock or seed for next year's crop, okay. That's what they needed to do to survive.

Obviously, some borrowers didn't like to hear that and didn't like to be turned down for a loan. Maybe they weren't happy, but people don't usually shoot their bankers. Maybe they think they'd like to, but they don't do it.

The death of John Hughes might have made me nervous, but not enough that it affected my daily work. Inflation and high interest rates were just a sign of the times. Customers knew it. Bankers knew it. Farmers knew it.

Somewhere in my career, probably when I was working for the government teaching agriculture courses to veterans in Johnson County after World War II, we did a comparison between the price of a gallon of milk and the cost of a gallon of beer. Milk was cheaper. Farmers might not have thought that was fair, but that's just the way it was.

Dairy farmers earn every penny they make. It's confining work. They're up early and to bed late. It's almost impossible to find somebody to fill in for you to take a vacation so it's seven days a week every week.

We need to be thankful the people out there enjoy what they're doing even though it's hard work.

Chapter 46

Ego, Greed and Jealousy

There's a popular picture of three monkeys in a row, one with his hands over his eyes, one with his hands over his ears and one with his hands over his mouth. The message is to see no evil, hear no evil, and speak no evil.

It also could easily be that you need to see that you keep your ego in check, ignore the greed you hear from others and do not speak aloud of your jealousy of others.

I'm a firm believer that these three human traits can cause more problems than any others. If everybody worked to keep them in check, it would be a much better world for business and for our personal lives.

You want everybody to like you. I don't know of anybody who doesn't want to be liked. That doesn't mean you want to be perfect. I've said some things I really regret. Some of them were long ago and I still remember them. You don't gain anything by saying it, but you do. People can find plenty of reasons not to like you without you giving them additional reasons.

One thing that really bugs me is that sometimes people intentionally do things to try to keep other people from succeeding. These people are just jealous. You don't raise yourself up by putting other people down. When you do that, it actually accomplishes

151

exactly the opposite and affects the way people view you.

As an example, I think about renting a farm out to a farmer. What I always try to remember is you need to let the farmer make a profit. Set the rent so it's fair and reasonable. If economic times mean you need to lower the rent, do it. If you've got a good farmer you want to keep him. The same goes for renting out a building, making a business loan and even working with a board of directors. Enable the others to succeed. It's all about being fair.

Greed isn't necessarily just trying to grab everything you can. In my opinion, it's also not being able to share what you have with others. It can be wealth, information, just reaching out to help someone else.

I know when it comes to greed that some people can't help it. If you have that particular characteristic, it's not going to be easy to change. But, when you share, you learn how good it feels and you see how it helps everybody out, including yourself.

This is the time in the conversation when I say that the guy who came up with "I, me and my" should be run out of town. It's not all about you. If you put others first, that can have the effect of putting you first in their eyes.

We all need a little ego. It drives motivation. But when it becomes excessive, it's hard for others to deal with. Sometimes you can't see it because you're too close – the forest for the trees syndrome – but other people see it. Even though other people don't say anything, it's on their minds and it becomes hard for them to let go of those thoughts whenever they're around you or think about you.

I'm reminded of the quote from Frank Leahy, the longtime and very successful football coach at Notre Dame. He said "Egotism is the anesthetic that dulls the pain of stupidity."

In other words, people with too much ego don't have enough sense to see how their stupidity causes pain for the people around them. There is so much ego around you get to the point you don't pay attention to it after a while, but it still causes plenty of problems.

Jealousy might be the root of both greed and ego. When you see someone who has more than you do – a tight-knit family, a lot of close friends, wealth, a better job, a higher position in the company, any number of things – you don't do anybody any favors, especially yourself, by putting the other person down.

The best way to overcome jealousy is to work your tail off to improve yourself, to step back and measure what you have today compared to what you had yesterday. If you've gotten a promotion, if you've made new friends, you're better off than you were. Again, it's all about integrity, thoughtfulness, being honest with yourself. Don't be jealous of others. Be happy with the way you are.

I learned so much about this from my mother. When I look back at her life, I am amazed that she could do so much and that she knew as much as she did with only an eighth-grade education. Howard Hall only had a tenth-grade education. You hope being around good people like this rubs off.

Chapter 47

Proud to be Czech

If people don't already know that I'm Czech through and through, I'll tell them. I don't make any excuses. When I look back at my family and relatives, I'm pretty proud of them. When you look at it, we were able to survive in a positive way during the Depression.

Five generations of Ernie Buresh's Czech heritage posed in 1944. Back row, left to right, are Ernie's father, Joe Buresh, his brother Lester holding daughter, Linda, and his mother, Emma. Front row, left to right, Mary Buresh (Joe's mother), Anna Becicka (Joe's Grandmother), Magdalene Houser (Emma's grandmother) and Barbara Stanek (Emma's mother).

I've been fortunate enough to explore my heritage back in the old country. The first time we went – Joanne, Wendy, Sandy and I – it wasn't a good time in the country's history. The Czech Republic was occupied by the Russians so we had to get there through Austria. We took a Czech airline to Prague and you could tell it was a depressed era – the stewardesses were wearing drab blue, they handed out hard candy and women hadn't shaved their legs.

We landed at this huge airport but inside the terminal there were only about 20 or 30 people milling around. We saw young Czechs leaving the country and their parents behind. It all seemed so empty.

After we hired a car to take us to the hotel, the driver kept trying to talk us into staying at another place. We had reservations at the Park Hotel, so that's where we needed to go. I kept insisting. I know how to speak Czech – my mother had us speak it all the time at home while we were growing up – so I was pretty convincing.

When we arrived, the elevators weren't working very well and we were hungry. In the restaurant, on the main floor, we ordered a fruit plate. It came with an apple, an orange, a banana and a knife to cut it up. After we ate we were able to ride the elevator up six stories to our room.

As we toured Prague, I came to realize that a beautiful big city didn't mean the people who lived there were happy. I would never forget the conversation I had with a cleaning lady at the hotel. She told me that if she was only younger, she'd leave the country in an instant.

This wasn't new to me, because relatives from Czechoslovakia, later the Czech Republic, had come to visit us in Iowa. Being in Prague made these feelings all the more real.

155

The Buresh family poses in 1971 for the 50th wedding anniversary of Joe and Emma Buresh, front. In the back row, left to right, are their children Les, Joan and Ernie.

My sister, Joan, had taken my mother to Pilsen in the Czech Republic to visit relatives, and those relatives, my mother's cousins, Miloslav and Dana Houser, visited us when we lived in Anamosa. They stayed with my mother in Shueyville while they were here. After a few days my mother confided in me that she was concerned they hadn't taken a bath yet. The customs were different in Europe. I told her to be subtle about it – to lay out a washcloth and a towel as a hint.

Miloslav was an engineer for the government, so he had a good job. He couldn't believe my mother was able to live in a house by herself. He and his wife lived in a government house.

My first conversations with Miloslav led me to believe he was a communist sympathizer. He acted like he believed the Russians were invited into the Czech Republic. But it didn't take him long over here to change his mind about that.

Again, I realized how fortunate I had been that my ancestors had come to Iowa. Growing up poor in the United States was a lot better than growing up in the middle class in Europe.

Chapter 48

Library Lessons

Having grown up poor, I'm a big believer in libraries. When you're poor, you have very limited access to the things a library can provide at no cost to you. Beyond that, in this current economic environment, it's a place young people can go, particularly for some of them who can't afford to have a computer and the Internet at home.

Joanne, my wife, is the reader in our family. She jokes with me that I never read books. I never got in the habit when I was young – it always seemed like there was work to do and the library wasn't very close to where I lived. Reading isn't a prerequisite to helping out a library. I joke back to Joanne that I can write. I can sign checks.

In the 1990s in Anamosa, the idea of a new library was just dangling. Everybody talked about it, but nobody did anything. We gave them the land for a new library and seed money to set up a matching contribution campaign. The community met the challenge to raise a million dollars on its own. With additional grant money we got the new library built and opened in 2004.

We were able to help Springville with its new library campaign, too. That led to the new building opening in 2005. The library already had the land so they didn't need that.

The Anamosa Public Library built on land donated by Ernie Buresh after he issued a $500,000 matching grant challenge.

In Anamosa, my brother Les and I bought the land east of the business district years before the library idea was even hatched because it was a good deal. One of those deals that's too hard to pass up.

I worshipped my brother for several reasons. Les was a hard worker, he had more friends than I ever did and he had great common sense and integrity. I tried to include him in everything I did and it worked out really well. He had enough funds to comfortably retire on when it came to that.

We were able to sell some of that land in Anamosa for the construction of the Casey's convenience store across from the Lawrence Community Center. Casey's later moved across Main Street and my longtime friend, Wayne Hall, the Chrysler dealer on the other side of Scott Street, bought the old Casey's. Since there was a strip of unused land between the old Casey's and the library, we gave that to Wayne because he's been so good to us through the years. We still buy our cars from him.

The old Remley mansion in Anamosa, which they tore down because it was too expensive to fix, had a library in it. I was able to save a walnut display case with glass doors. After having it at our house for a while, we donated it to the Anamosa library and dedicated it to Howard Remley and his wife, Betty. Howard was a highly respected lawyer and they had taken us by the hand when we were new to Anamosa so that it seemed as if we'd been there all along. People who knew them or knew of them enjoy seeing their pictures there.

When the new library was built in Anamosa, never once did anyone ask for my opinion on the new building. To be honest, that was disappointing. It hurt my feelings. All they wanted from me was to put together information on what I gave them. I didn't respond. I wasn't about to do that, to blow my own horn.

When I think back on that, I think about how Howard Hall was my mentor. He learned an awful lot through his life, from his experiences. I was always asking Mr. Hall for advice. That didn't mean I'd follow everything he said to the letter. Absolutely not. He never expected me to do that. But he appreciated being asked and when he saw what I did, he knew I was paying attention.

The Springville library was completely different. It's smaller than the one in Anamosa, but I was able to see the plans all along the process. Building a library is like building anything – it's a costly item and you need to have a business plan. Springville did that. What I like about their library is that it has a fireplace. You can curl up there to read a book.

Libraries are great places for learning, but they aren't the only places. You learn a lot by talking to mentors in your life, by listening to what they have to say. Learn from other people's mistakes so you don't make the same ones. That's common sense.

Using other people's experiences can give you a great education.

Ernie Buresh stands in the fireplace reading area, his favorite room at the Springville Public Library.

Chapter 49

Be Glad to Pay Your Taxes

George Paulsen, the Onslow banker who became my father-in-law, used to say, "Never complain about paying taxes. If I pay taxes, then I know I'm doing okay."

In other words, he was earning enough money that he had to pay income taxes. And I agree with that to a certain extent. If it was a perfect world, paying taxes would be a pleasure. If it were a perfect world you'd pay your taxes, they would be spent properly and you'd get your benefits back. Unfortunately, it's not a perfect world.

In my opinion, the more governments tax us, the more they spend without considering the difference between needs and wants.

There we go again. It's easy to spend somebody else's money on things you want when you know you can get more money from them. If we had a common sense approach to the needs and wants of government, it would sure reduce the need for tax money that we spend. But, we keep expanding government and we need to get the money for that somewhere.

What's the problem with having reserves? I agree with Gov. Terry Branstad that we don't need to spend it all on wants. It's such a simple approach. But it reverts back to the mentality of the electorate. It's simple budgeting. If you don't budget, how do you know what you need and where you're at with your expenditures? And what happens when you have unexpected expenses? You borrow money and pay interest.

This was a big thing during my banking career. I was surprised how many people came in for loans without a budget or without a business plan. They probably had an idea in their minds but we had to help them get it down on paper.

When you look around we pay a lot of taxes – property tax, sales tax, gas tax, cable TV tax, sin taxes on alcohol and tobacco – but I'm mostly talking about income tax.

When it comes to the roads, I'm not a fan of toll roads. Then again, that tax is paid for by people who use the roads and that's similar to the way the gas tax works. You buy gas to drive on the roads, so you pay for their upkeep. Somebody has to pay for it.

With income taxes, corporations take advantage of loopholes, yet they get a lot of advantages for regular tax breaks. A flat tax has been proposed to cut out loopholes. That makes a lot of sense to me, but everybody wants to make even that complicated, so it doesn't pass.

But, why shouldn't the tax be the same for everybody? There's so much cheating on taxes. I'm not sure I understand everything about a flat tax, but if it works like people say it would, we'd be better off with it than we are now.

There's so much talk about helping the middle class and that's fine. That's exactly the point of this book.

When I was growing up we were poor, but we never relied on welfare. Why has there been so much expansion of welfare? The sad part is, the easier you make it to take advantage of welfare, the harder it is for people to succeed.

That's because, once people get on welfare, they aren't going to work if they don't have to. It's hard to get away from the idea that you can get something for nothing. It's human nature, but it's not a wise thing to subscribe to. That's part of the workings of politics, that people on welfare will vote for politicians who support these programs because they don't want to give up that meal ticket. Once you get on that welfare bus, it's hard to get off.

This all fits into trying to explain what's wrong with our country today. There is no shame in growing up poor; you can help yourself out of it if you want to. There are so many ways to fix government, but they're impossible to implement because there's no desire from the people in government to do it.

Chapter 50

Community Banks

Face New Threats

The last sixty-percent of the Twentieth Century, in my opinion, was much better for the community banking industry than any of the periods before that and, it appears, in the period they're facing now. For that, I feel blessed to have had my entire working career take place in what I consider the best of times.

Banks ran into trouble soon after I was born. The stock market crash of 1929, The Great Depression, trying to get out of that until World War II. That's when the economy picked up and community banks saw the benefit. People trusted them again.

In the newspaper the other day I saw where a credit union was advertising car loans at 2.49 percent interest. That was unheard of in my day. Banks are hardly paying anything for money any more, but when rates are that low it means their margins have to be lower than they used to be.

I don't know that I should be talking about banking today because I'm from a different era. I don't know if I was a good banker or not. I can't compare the environment I was in to the one today.

But, I've seen some changes that concern me when it comes to community banks. These are the banks that grew up in a community and served that community and had that community return the loyalty.

Today, you see a bank on every corner. Or it's a credit union. Regulations have changed and rules are different.

The Bank Office Bill of more than a decade ago relaxed the rules on where banks can have offices. At one time banks were restricted to having them in adjacent counties but that's no longer the case. You now sees banks around that you've never heard of before.

Credit Unions, on the other hand, have a completely different set of rules and regulations. They started as a service to employees of businesses, corporations, even universities. Now, pretty much anybody can become a member of any credit union.

Credit unions don't pay income taxes and they don't have the security of the FDIC (Federal Deposit Insurance Corporation) to guarantee that your savings are safe.

Are these changes killing community banks? I think they are. It's a lot more difficult for them to compete than it used to be which is unfortunate for the communities. I'm just glad I'm an ex-banker.

Chapter 51

Religion and Politics

Don't Mix with Business

I grew up as a Czech protestant, but most of my friends were Czech Catholic. I'm a Republican, but most of my friends are Democrats.

Does this mean opposites attract? Hardly. It's just an observation and nothing more. I bring it up only because I've never judged relationships by what people believe when it comes to religion and politics. I'm much more concerned about their personalities and how they think about other things in life.

Religion is important, but it's your own. I believe in God and that Jesus was the son of God. If you don't believe in God, how do you justify the four seasons, the grass growing, an afterlife?

My parents didn't go to church but I occasionally went to the United Brethren Church (it's now a Methodist church) in Shueyville for Sunday school. Later, when I was more high school age, I enjoyed Christian Endeavor on Sunday evenings at the Bohemian and Moravian Brethren Church near Ely.

Religion was really a small part of it. The social aspect is what attracted me, being with ten or twelve friends that were different from high school friends since they came from a larger area.

Since I wasn't baptized as a youngster, I had myself baptized at the Ely church while on leave from the Army. Joanne and I also attended the church after we married and had some good times. We were active among the young adults, attended square dances and I served as an elder. It's where both Wendy and Sandy were baptized as babies.

In Anamosa we attended the United Methodist Church and after we moved to Cedar Rapids we joined the First Presbyterian Church.

When it comes to politics, my dad was a Democrat. My mother never talked about politics much. That's how smart she was.

My parents voted regularly and I remember voting as soon as I was old enough. I've never been heavily involved in politics, but I enjoy keeping up with it in the news. Even though I'm a registered Republican, I've voted for Democrats. I don't like to tell anybody how I voted unless I have to and then I'll be honest. You need to listen to both sides. But, to me, the Republican Party has become disappointing of late.

Politics in general are going in the wrong direction. The welfare of the country doesn't seem to be an important issue for either party. In my opinion, it's all about getting re-elected and accumulating wealth. There ought to be term limits. At least make them get out for a couple of years.

The other day, while playing bridge, some of my friends were talking negatively about Joni Ernst, the new Republican U.S. Senator from Iowa. She was smart enough to get elected, but I didn't say anything. It wouldn't do any good. You can't change their minds.

I think it's counterproductive to talk about religion and politics in the process of developing relationships. We just need a simple understanding that you have your views and I have mine. That's great. Now, what else do you want to talk about?

168

Chapter 52

Rise and Shine

I can still get up at four in the morning and not worry about it. I just like to get up early. It's the best time of the day. There aren't a lot of interruptions. Let the other people sleep. I can get a lot done and then I can look forward to slowing down a little in the afternoon.

I've told you why I think I'm weird. I've never made a home mortgage payment. I've never worn a wrist watch. I never read the funnies. I don't use an alarm clock.

For some reason, my body has always been aware of time. If I ever needed an exact time, I always had a buddy who wore a watch.

But I've never needed an alarm clock. I can set my mind. Then, I'm up way before any alarm would go off. I can't remember being late very often. If I'm going to be late, I call. My secretary had a wonderful tickler system so she made sure I kept my calendar of appointments up to date.

Of course, when you get up early, you go to bed early. When I was working out of a briefcase, to visit the banks, I'd probably be in bed by nine and then up before six. You need at least eight hours of sleep. Now it's probably closer to nine-thirty or ten when I go to bed and I might be up by five. And, that's every night and every day. When you're used to getting up early, the day of the week doesn't change anything.

To be honest, I loved my work and never really looked forward to vacations. Certainly, as a family, we were fortunate to be able to travel a lot. But, to me, vacations were a family duty – something you did for your family. I always enjoyed seeing the girls have a good time. That was vacation for me.

So, yes, I may not have the banks anymore, but I don't know that I'm retired. There are still plenty of things to do around the house early in the morning. That keeps you young.

Maybe I'm retired, but I'm still working. If you don't stay busy, life would be a total bore.

Chapter 53

Philanthropy

is its Own Reward

If you are able to help good people who need your help, you should do it, no questions asked. You should do it without expecting anything in return. Just the idea that you've done something nice is its own reward. That's how philanthropy works.

Philanthropy is more important today than ever. People who can afford to do it need to contribute to their favorite causes. Unfortunately, there's a lot of money wasted in philanthropy and that's the bad part. But, there's so much good, too. It goes back to what my mother always said – what you give away comes back twice. But I'm not talking about the money angle, I'm talking about the feeling you get knowing you've improved something you really believe in and our society as a whole.

Howard Hall showed me first-hand how important philanthropy can be. How many people's lives have been saved or at least improved since the 1950s because of the Hall Radiation Center at Mercy Hospital? There's the foundation he set up that helps so many causes today and will help long into the future.

Just look around and there are so many other examples. At the University of Iowa you see evidence of the great gifts from Marvin Pomerantz, John Pappajohn and Henry Tippie. But there are so many others on various scales whose contributions are just as important to the university. The amount of a gift isn't as important as giving at least something.

I learned a lot about philanthropy from Herman Schmidt who was president of the University of Iowa Foundation when I became involved. He and his wife, Eileen, both graduated from the University of Iowa and he later graduated from Harvard Law School. He was a vice-chairman of Mobil Oil and gave money to the University of Iowa for 45 years. After he died, his estate left $1 million to the university.

As a lifetime trustee at Cornell College in Mount Vernon I've also seen wonderful philanthropic efforts, although on a different scale than at the University of Iowa. They have a much smaller pool to draw from, but it's all needed.

There are so many worthwhile causes that will always need financial assistance. Find one, step up and make your contribution. Philanthropy is necessary from generation to generation for our society to prosper.

Chapter 54

The Death of a Mentor

Howard Hall's death in 1971 not only shocked me, but it filled me with a lot of sadness. He was such a great man, a great friend, a great mentor to me and so many other people. You expected him to live forever.

The last time we talked we had a reasonable conversation. He'd always had a problem with asthma and he hadn't been feeling well.

Howard's funeral at Brucemore was attended by hundreds of people from all walks of life. We filed past Howard's open casket but I didn't want to remember him that way. I know I wasn't alone. The one thing I'll always remember about that day was seeing a former board member of City National Bank, one that Howard had diplomatically convinced to resign, out on the lawn directing traffic after the funeral. Despite the conflict, this man was totally devoted to Howard and they remained friends. That was the magic of Howard Hall.

The idea was to carry on as Howard would want. That's what I did at City National and as a board member of his Iowa Manufacturing Company, although it certainly wasn't the same. Howard's death created a void. I had lost someone to talk to, to confide in. It's so sad it's hard to explain. Howard had such a great manner, a tremendous amount of plain old common sense. When I saw how complete it was in

173

him, maybe that's how I came up with the idea that truly, common sense is anything but common.

Joanne and I had been good friends of the Halls and we kept that relationship going with Margaret for the next ten years until her death in 1981. She had handled Howard's death well and appreciated having us to confide in as well as their longtime employees Carolyn Shimek and Nile (the butler).

Joanne Buresh chats with Howard and Margaret Hall in front of their Palisades cottage in May, 1970.

In a way Howard and Margaret live on through the Hall Foundation he established several years before his death. I am amazed at how many organizations

174

that has helped, how many millions of dollars of good it has done for the community and Eastern Iowa.

Howard asked me to serve on the Hall Foundation board along with a half-dozen others that included John Turner, the funeral home director and friend of Grant Wood. It has been more than an honor. It's a way to keep the Hall wishes alive. It's a commitment and I'm so glad to do it. It's a lifetime appointment. I could resign but I'm not going to because of my belief in what Howard wanted. It's a lifetime commitment.

Howard and Margaret Hall are buried at Oak Hill Cemetery in Cedar Rapids. They left me the key to their mausoleum so I check it periodically.

A lot of great people from Cedar Rapids are buried at Oak Hill. The cemetery has run into financial difficulties of late and I tried to get the Hall Foundation to donate funds to help it out because I think that's what Howard would want. But the rules don't allow the foundation to donate to the cemetery and, apparently, we can't change that.

Yes, I know the foundation is technically the Hall-Perrine Foundation now. But I still think of it as Howard's and Margaret's legacy.

I've talked before about how close Joanne and I were to the Halls, particularly when we'd be with them at their Palisades cottage on a bluff overlooking the Cedar River across from Palisades-Kepler State Park east of Cedar Rapids. Still, I was shocked when the Halls left us the cottage in their wills.

Joanne and I took Margaret to the cottage often. It was a nice, quiet place to get away, that stone-walled cottage with its high peaked roof built in the 1930s. It sat on 53 acres that once had a pheasant run and places for chickens, deer and a pet mule of Howard's.

When we inherited the cottage after Margaret's death, I had the old caretaker's home torn down and replaced. We used the area often, but not so much after 2000. We donated it to help build the new hospital in Anamosa – it was sold with the funds going to that project.

Joanne and I knew that's what Howard would have wanted. Remember, he was a Jones County boy, having grown up in Onslow where Joanne also grew up. It was pretty amazing that we had that connection.

I can't imagine how different my life would have been without Howard Hall. I have always felt lucky and blessed, never more so than to have known Howard.

Howard and Margaret Hall's Palisades cottage.

Friends, Family and Fun

Chapter 55

Success

When you first think about defining success, you most likely think of financial gains. Some people stop there. You can't. You've got to think of all of the ways you can be successful.

The way I see it, success is achieving the goals you set for yourself in three areas – business, education and personal. Working toward these goals you develop integrity, truthfulness and loyalty. If you accomplish all of these goals, in your business life, in pursuing your education, in nurturing your personal life – which we're talking about extensively in this book – you're successful.

You absolutely mustn't forget your family. You have to do the right things for your family so everything around them turns into a positive.

As I was growing up on the farms and in Western, I kind of felt like I was out there by myself. It's lonely. It's always lonely when you're young and live on a farm. You don't have a lot of contact with other people.

But, as I grew older, I realized how important family had been.

My brother teased me because he didn't want his younger brother around. He was four years older. But my brother was so very important in my life.

I looked up to my uncle Lou, an elementary teacher in Konigsmark out near what is the Eastern Iowa

Airport, because he was smart and always made sense to me when he'd answer my questions.

Georgia Stotts and Lou Buresh, Ernie Buresh's aunt and uncle on his father's side, in 1984.

And, of course, my mother. She was my earliest mentor and her ideals, her philosophies about how you should live your life, have stayed with me forever. So, I guess I wasn't so much alone, not like I'd thought.

In trying to define success, we could be here all day. I think it all comes down to accomplishing personal goals because that leads to success in reaching your business and educational goals. Your personal development – surrounding yourself with the best family members and the greatest friends – provides you with close relationships that not only give you the opportunity to keep learning, but allow you to teach other people what you know. That is a powerful incentive to motivate anyone to become a success.

Does luck play a role in success? Certainly. But you create your own opportunities. When you do that and wind up in the right place at the right time, some people might see that as purely luck. You know better. You know it was a combination of luck and hard work.

Have I been successful? In some things, probably. I was successful in getting through college, but that doesn't mean anything except I did it. I bought some banks. That doesn't mean anything. But at a bank I've been able to help other people reach their goals, to see their dreams come true, and I'd say that's success.

Motivation is a key element. It's hard if you're out there alone. That's why, sometimes, people give up too soon. Surround yourself with good people, develop important relationships, help others out and they'll help you. Just keep at it, set your goals and go for them. There are so many steps in success. Take them one at a time. You'll get there.

Chapter 56

Observations:

Getting to Know Ernie

From the beginning when I sat down with Ernie Buresh to find out what makes him tick, I could see that helping him write his book was going to be an educational, enlightening and entertaining adventure. As the days, weeks, and months progressed, Ernie didn't disappoint. Every conversation fit the bill – something learned, something new, something fun.

Not only did I relish what Ernie had to say next, but I got a kick out of his facial expressions. He'd raise his white eyebrows above the dark frames of his glasses, open his eyes wide to create creases in his forehead, scrunch up his nose, lean forward and say something like, "Can you believe it?" He'd sit back in his chair, remove his glasses and close his eyes as if to fall asleep, only he was just trying to picture a memory going through his mind. With pen poised over the print on a page, he'd shake his head, draw his lips tight against his teeth, narrow his eyebrows and say "We don't want to say this that way."

In one of the early interviews, Ernie made a claim that I doubted, that I know covered my face with a puzzled expression. When he caught my quizzical look, he said matter-of-factly, "I just made that up."

After we laughed, Ernie explained that Margaret Hall, the wife of Cedar Rapids entrepreneur Howard Hall, used that expression when she'd say something she didn't mean, something she wanted to take back. It always added levity to the moment.

A sense of humor can get you a long way.

Several months into the interviews, Ernie had played bridge with friends one morning and opened our conversation by saying he had embarrassed himself. Like Margaret Hall, he'd said something he wanted to take back. "You need to learn to keep your mouth shut," he said. "I apologized for what I said. 'That was really a stupid thing to say.' But by then it was too late."

Yep. People won't automatically erase what you said when you apologize. But you need to apologize anyway.

Ernie was a Boy Scout as a kid. He learned the organization's basics – be honest, loyal, trustworthy, truthful, helpful, courteous, clean, thrifty, kind – all things his mother had instilled in him. But Ernie's participation didn't last long. The main reason: he was a country kid among city kids. "It wasn't much fun," he said. "I was never at ease playing with city kids, partly because it seemed that they had so much more as far as experiences went. I felt inferior."

Being humble is one thing; not fitting in is entirely different.

Many a time Ernie wondered if he should be putting together a book. "I'm just a Mr. Nobody," he'd say. He decided to do it with the urging of friends through the years. And he'd list some of those friends – movers and shakers and decisions makers of their communities (many of whom are mentioned in this book) – and he'd say, "When you see what these people have accomplished, it makes you proud to be their friend."

185

Other times, after he'd peruse the first draft of another chapter, Ernie would smile. "Even if nobody reads this book, it's been worth it," he'd say.

The exercise has convinced Ernie that everybody is somebody. It has given him the opportunity to discuss lifetime philosophies. He's been able to praise people he admires. And it has taxed his memory – a great memory for details and quotes – to the point that he sometimes wondered if a date or a detail he remembered is actually the way it was.

"Go ask Joanne," he'd occasionally say. "She'll remember that part."

Or, Ernie might simply smile and scrunch up his eyebrows. "Put down after that," he'd joke, "I just made that up."

Dave Rasdal

Chapter 57

Drinking Doesn't Mean a Good Time

My mother always encouraged me to get out and meet new people. That's why I enjoyed going to dances most every night when I could, both when I was in high school and after my days in the service. It's why I've played cards for decades. Why I'd get involved in community activities like the Grant Wood Art Festival.

Some of the stories I'd hear about the horse and buggy days, when my great-grandparents' house out in the country had its own indoor dance floor that brought in people from miles around, always fascinated me. In my day, though, we had the ballrooms in Cedar Rapids. Danceland, CeMar, Armar. Joanne and I had our first date at DanceMor in Swisher.

One thing I learned early was that a lot of people thought you had to drink alcohol to have a good time at the dances. I never developed a taste for it. It wasn't only because of my dad. I didn't like to see him drunk. But anytime I'd see somebody else drunk, it was a real turnoff. Besides that, there's the cost.

Don't get me wrong, I've got a closet full of liquor for guests. I've never tried to tell anybody not to drink. I've

187

never decided who I'd be friends with based on whether they drank or not. It was their business.

Soft drinks were always good enough for me at the dances. That way I'd remember the people I'd meet. I enjoyed the dancing, even though I didn't know that much about it at first. I just picked it up from girls I danced with.

I'm all for having a good time, but for too many people that's all they want, just a good time. Meeting new people, that's what it's all about.

Chapter 58

Living a Long Life

Take care of your health.

There. I said it. Now, go out and eat a big juicy steak.

Nobody likes to have somebody preach at them about getting enough exercise and sleep, about not drinking and smoking, about eating your vegetables and avoiding sweets.

We all know what's right. That's my point. Take care of yourself.

When you're born poor, you don't go to the dentist like you should because you can't afford it. You don't go to the doctor for the same reason. But cleanliness shouldn't be a problem.

I still feel a chill up my back from climbing into the galvanized tub on weekly bath nights and having my back hit that cold metal. The water was warm – my mother had heated it on the stove – and soapy. I had a bar of soap, too. It was kind of like doing the dishes. But it was a lot of work which is why I think we only did it once a week.

Whenever I'd get sick, which was very rare, my mother always had some way to get me back on my feet. But the point was, even though we were poor, I got plenty of exercise and ate right.

In addition to my genes, the longevity I've had, to some extent, has to be credited to my diet when I was growing up. We always had plenty to eat. That's the advantage of living on a farm and of having a mother who liked to tend a big garden and raise chickens.

I still love fried chicken. Also, scrambled eggs and fried potatoes were a regular breakfast when I was growing up.

I've always eaten breakfast to start the day. When I was in the banks, I'd fix it myself because I'd get up so early I didn't want Joanne to have to get up and do it. I fixed oatmeal a lot.

Recently, when I was in pain and waiting to get my hip replaced, nothing tasted good. I seldom eat cold cereal. But, around that time, I put some Special K in a bowl with some blueberries and nuts and poured milk over it and heated it all up in the microwave. It was delicious.

There are a lot of things I really like to eat. Asparagus, white cod and salmon prepared certain ways. I even like sardines and ice cream, but there's nothing like a good steak.

I always think about the Hall cottage when I'm asked how I want my steak done. Howard Hall grilled the steaks and he'd come in to ask how we wanted them cooked. We'd tell him and he'd go outside to fix them. Then his wife, Margaret, would laugh and say, "He always asks that question and the steaks are always the same."

One thing I rarely eat is gravy. The reason I don't is that I've observed cooks who dip the ladle into it and, you know, taste it and put the ladle back. It's a cleanliness thing with me.

Ask Joanne. We can pull up to a restaurant and if I don't like the way it looks, we won't stop. Or, we'll go inside and I see something that I don't like, something that doesn't look clean, and we'll get up and leave. A clean kitchen is important to me.

I may have grown up poor and we didn't have anything fancy to eat, but my mother always kept her kitchen clean. She lived to be 97. You figure it out.

Emma Buresh, Ernie's mother, holds one of her rag rugs as she sits by the wood box inside the refurbished Blacksmith Shop in Stone City.

Chapter 59

Loving a Special Child

We did all we could for Sandy, but it was never as much as she did for us. We could never love her as much as she loved us.

Sandy was an incredible child. Every parent should feel that way no matter what challenges their child might face. Joanne was a saint with Sandy. All she did was love her. Joanne did everything she could and they were such buddies.

I remember after Sandy's first heart surgery, how she came home and was just like any child back in the neighborhood and at school. She had her friends, but nobody as close as the Holets sisters – Chris, Vicky and Julie – in Swisher. Sandy wrote to them her entire life. We still hear from them.

Always, it was evident that Sandy was smart. There was nothing wrong with her brain. It was just that, with her speech impediment and being so small, some people couldn't see that. But Sandy never thought of herself as having any handicap. She was a child who had needs and she grew into an adult who had needs. We can all say that about ourselves.

In the third grade, Sandy was a very happy child until her teacher left in the middle of the school year. She missed that teacher so it was hard. Then, in the fourth grade, she had trouble with her math. When the teacher suggested we hold her back a year, we thought it was the right thing to do. But, it was devastating to Sandy. For a while she acted like she didn't care about anything.

Now, this was a time of one of my most incredible regrets.

In Anamosa, Sandy rode the school bus to Morley. We thought everything was fine until Joanne gave her a bath one night. That's when Joanne noticed little black and blue dots on Sandy's skin. We wondered what that was all about until Sandy told us that a boy on the bus would jab his pencil through the opening in the seat into her back.

I always grew up with the idea that you had to let your child handle any problems with their classmates on their own. We just let it go. Sandy had the brains to figure it out, but she wasn't strong enough. The problem finally went away. But I've since changed my mind one-hundred-eighty degrees about this.

If you have a child who needs special attention, you need to do everything you can for that child. This was bullying. I would have given that bully kid a real shakedown. He'd never do that again.

Sandy had other challenges with people her own age, too. After her second heart surgery, she was found to have scoliosis, a curvature of the spine. She had to wear a Milwaukee Brace, a metal apparatus that goes outside of the clothes to support her neck, spine and hips. Apparently, this was not unusual when the breastbone had been separated because the spine was susceptible to curvature. She had to wear the brace 23 hours a day through junior high school. The kids, of course, looked at her differently and would tease her about it.

But Sandy was stronger than a lot of people gave her credit for. Children can be resilient.

Sandy once wrote to William Shatner who was in one of her favorite TV shows, "Star Trek," and got a picture back from him. That's also when she began to watch The Rev. Robert Schuller and would write to him.

Sandy Buresh was thrilled to meet her idol, The Rev. Dr. Robert Schuller, on a visit to his Crystal Cathedral in Garden Grove, California, with her parents Joanne and Ernie.

I know that Sandy wasn't able to do some of the things her friends did. She couldn't take swimming lessons because we couldn't risk her getting a cold because of the surgeries. When she'd go to a friend's house for an overnight party, Joanne would pick her up about ten at night and bring her home for the  same reasons. But Sandy never complained.

Sandy also had a mischievous side when it came to being a little sister. She'd set up her tape recorder to spy on Wendy and her friends when they were at the house which irritated Wendy.

Sometimes we wondered if Wendy resented Sandy for all of the attention she got, but Wendy was able to do what she wanted to do, too, so she says that was never the case. The summer Joanne drove Sandy to the University of Iowa for speech therapy nearly every day, Wendy took typing and swimming lessons. This was just sisters being sisters.

That's what we loved about Sandy. She missed a lot in her life, which is part of the reason we took so many trips. She spent a lot of time with Joanne, so a lot of her friends were older. But when she had a good time, you knew it and she knew it. Her smile could light up the room.

Sandy Buresh and her good friend, Kay Bernau, pose for the camera in 1997.

Chapter 60

Mr. Camp Courageous

When I first met Charlie Becker I was impressed with his friendliness and the way he made everyone feel special. That's exactly what you'd expect from the director of Camp Courageous, the camp outside Monticello that helps special needs people of all ages. But Charlie is much more than that.

We got to know each other better when he came to me at the Anamosa bank to help set up the foundation for Camp Courageous. I had followed Camp Courageous, not only because it was in Jones County, but because I was impressed more than anything else with how the camp could become such a success without government money. It is solely funded by individual and corporate contributions.

Charlie Becker, director of Camp Courageous.

In my experience, keeping those contributions coming in is one of the most difficult challenges every non-profit faces. But, in the final analysis, it always boils down to one person and the people he surrounds himself with.

Charlie Becker is Camp Courageous. He's such a perfect example of the definition of success. He works tirelessly for the camp every day, all day. He gives more than 100 percent because he believes in it 100 percent. His thoughtfulness is astounding. He is concerned not only for every camper, but for all of the people involved with the camp beyond the campers.

Our daughter, Sandy, was never a camper at Camp Courageous. She never saw herself as having a handicap – her brain was fine but her speech was slow and hard for others to understand. She knew how much good the camp did for kids who needed it. And she liked Charlie.

Lately, Charlie has been able to help Joanne and me with our downsizing. When something we no longer need would work at the camp, we're more than happy to donate it.

You can't help but wonder what Camp Courageous would have been like today without Charlie Becker. You wonder what it will be like after he retires. He is so much Camp Courageous and deserves all of the credit you could ever give anyone.

Chapter 61

Wendy Becomes a Doctor

When Wendy said she wanted to become a doctor, we said fine. There was no long discussion about it. When your child says "I'm going to be a doctor" you certainly don't say "No."

Joanne and I always encouraged her to be whatever she wanted to be. I tried to talk almost anybody I knew out of becoming a lawyer. Wendy didn't want that. I didn't even try to push banking onto her.

Wendy Buresh about the time she graduated from medical school at the University of Iowa.

Banking is a unique profession – you either have it or you don't. There are a lot of people in banking who don't have it. But I loved it. That's the key to success. If you have a problem going to work, then that's a really big problem.

Wendy and Sandy were very different from each other. So much of Sandy's life revolved around her health issues. Wendy didn't have that, but she had to deal with her own wants and needs, how to balance those out and still be the best big sister she could be. With Sandy's medical issues, it seemed natural that Wendy would want to be a doctor.

Wendy took her undergraduate work at Cornell College in Mount Vernon and was able to combine her senior year there with her first year of medical school at the University of Iowa. She served her family medicine residency in Des Moines and for more than thirty years now has had her own practice in Cedar Rapids.

She knew that's what she wanted all along because she works best on her own. "Dad," she told me once, "I don't play well with others." We still laugh about that.

Wendy and her husband, Alan Robb, a retired doctor, have two children, Kate and T.J. Kate is a pediatrician at University Hospitals and just began a fellowship in pediatric intensive care at the University of Iowa. T.J. is a maintenance engineer at the Doubletree Inn in downtown Cedar Rapids. It has been nice to have her family so close all the time.

T.J. hasn't had the easiest time of it, but I'm so proud of him now. He was diagnosed with Asperger's Syndrome (an autism spectrum disorder) and has had a number of social struggles. But he has worked hard to be successful and even bought his own home. He lives with his fiancée and seems to be getting along. Joanne and I have received phone calls from out of the blue where people tell us he's in jail and they need money to bail him out. He's not anywhere near jail – these are just unscrupulous people who hear about something and try to take advantage of it. We just hang up the phone.

It's easy to see that Wendy has a great relationship with her children. But she has great relationships with everybody, especially her patients. She's a family practice physician so she sees patients of all ages with all types of medical issues.

If Wendy was money-oriented, she'd see that she spends too much time with her patients. But she's not. She didn't become a doctor to make money. She has a huge regard for the humanitarian delivery of medicine for the good of every single patient. That's why she became a doctor and she's never forgotten that. This was the right decision for Wendy. You couldn't be more proud of a daughter.

Chapter 62

Character Shines

Through at Early Age

Sometimes you spot a person's character early in his life, and that's how it was about fifty years ago after we'd moved to Anamosa. It was the 1960s when I crossed paths with a young man whose ambition and common sense shined above other kids his age. That's how Rick Stickle and I became friends for life.

I'm not sure when Rick first came to me to be his banker, but he was always tossing around ideas to become an entrepreneur. Anything he'd come up with showed that his plans were well-thought through. He'd learned about the salvage business from his grandfather, Ben Stickle, who saved old lumber, and Rick was able to build it up into a successful venture for himself.

Beyond that, Rick became involved in other businesses that included the purchase of railroad right-of-way out of the Rock Island Railroad bankruptcy in the 1980s. He wound up with about 12,000 acres and another 1,500 linear miles of right-of-way. I'd imagine he was the largest private land owner in Iowa at one time.

When Rick talked to me about acquiring that railroad land, it took a lot of money but I knew it would work. I didn't see how it could fail, except for mismanagement, and that wasn't going to happen with Rick. I already had enough experience with him to know that his management was an asset, not a liability.

Much of Rick's business has also been in warehousing, which goes right along with the salvage business. He owns the old Army Depot grounds in Savanna, Ill. which includes about 100 buildings he uses as warehouse space.

Rick Stickle, a long-time friend of Ernie Buresh's, sits at his desk in the replica railroad depot he built in Cedar Rapids.

Rick was in the international shipping business for a while, too, and owned several ocean-going vessels. But he got out of that after he was wrongly convicted of illegally dumping contaminated grain and had to spend three years in federal prison.

What happened was that Rick ran the business from Cedar Rapids and trusted the people he hired to oversee the hands-on part of the operation. His ships would haul grain to the Mideast and bring oil back. When oil got into one of the grain shipments, the man in charge of the ship illegally dumped it in the ocean. Rick didn't know anything about it until two weeks later and even then the ship's captain lied and said the Coast Guard had approved the dumping. Rick was the fall guy because it was his business.

The public should judge for themselves if Rick ever deserved to serve even one day, because there was no evidence, written or oral, that implicated him. I know that a lot of people supported Rick. District Judge Dave Remley of Anamosa, now retired, is a longtime friend and gave Rick a lot of personal support through the ordeal even though he couldn't do anything from a legal standpoint.

Just to show Rick's character, he paid the fines and served the sentence. He refused to make a deal with the government because he didn't do anything wrong. It was a matter of principle.

He served his time at the federal prison in Oxford, Wisconsin, where I visited him once. All of the time he was there, he made every loan payment on time, without fail. Not only that, but he became a law clerk and helped another man get six months off of his sentence because he felt it was the right thing to do.

For those reasons and many more, Rick is incredible. Every time I have a problem, he wants to fix it. He constantly checks on me to see how I'm doing. When it was hard for me to get out with my painful hip, his wife, Marsha, came over to the house to give me a haircut. He's sent other people out to remove trees and other things on the property. He's always ready to do a favor.

We often talk about Rick's projects. He'll pick me up and we go for a drive to see what he's got going, to see what we need to do to make it work. I'll ask him for advice, too, when it comes to personal decisions I need to make like selling my original farm.

I really want to give Rick the credit he deserves. He's a very caring and giving person. He doesn't have a formal education beyond high school but he's become very successful.

Of all the people I've met, Rick Stickle and Howard Hall stand out as having the most common sense, a business common sense. It's something you're born with, but it's also something you've got to develop through personal integrity and experience.

Chapter 63

Sandy Becomes an Adult

After Sandy finished the tenth grade in Anamosa, she didn't want to go back to school there. After the bullying, her mental health became a big concern. A Dubuque psychiatrist suggested she try the Brown School in San Marcos, Texas, which is near Austin. Joanne and I agreed, even though we knew we'd miss her.

When Sandy visited the school, she really liked what she saw with the buildings, the dorms and the people. In particular, Sandy liked a counselor there and knew it was the place for her. But that counselor moved on, so after Sandy celebrated her 16th birthday in Texas, she came home.

We thought Sandy was old enough to make up her own mind, so I gave her a job at the bank in Anamosa. She filed checks, changed the dates on the calendars, visited with customers. She enjoyed getting a paycheck and loved her mother very much, so every payday she'd go to the flower shop next door and visit with Don Bunce and later Peggy Walton. These visits and buying a flower for her mom were so important and a joy for her.

Even though she quit working at the bank when we moved to Cedar Rapids, she kept up with her Anamosa friends. Joanne would take her to Tucker's Tavern where Sandy would drink her Pepsi, listen to the juke box and visit. Every week she'd have her hair done by Sheryl Owen at Guys and Gals. She'd bring homemade treats for everyone. Sandy followed this ritual for the rest of her life.

As an adult, after moving to Cedar Rapids, Sandy enjoyed a monthly trip to Iowa City to see Kay Bernau who had founded a Red Hat Society chapter, so they called themselves "The Red Hots." Theresa Marlowe and Janelle Parks were fantastic friends in Cedar Rapids. They'd take Sandy on all-day outings throughout Eastern Iowa. She treasured those trips even though she fought increasing fatigue as her heart began to wear out.

As much as anything, Sandy loved nature – hills and mountains, sure, but mostly flowers and butterflies. She loved to be surrounded by the beauty around her which only helped to make her more beautiful inside.

I don't know of anyone who was more generous. She was happiest when she gave something away that put a smile on your face. That's how Joanne, Wendy and I know that, on special occasions, when we see a Monarch butterfly, it has been sent to us by Sandy.

Sandy Buresh smiles as she takes a short break from work at the Citizens Savings Bank in Anamosa in the early 1970s.

Chapter 64

A Great Dane

Sometimes when you venture into new territory you get more than you bargained for and that can be a good thing. When I purchased the bank in Springville, I met Paul Nielsen who farmed southwest of town and still does, even though he's in his 80s.

As we set about fixing up the bank, we learned that Paul had been building houses. We asked him about doing some work on the bank and, pretty soon after that, put him on the payroll. In my opinion, Paul is a construction genius, without reservation.

A lot of that, of course, comes because he has tremendous common sense. But, he's also Danish and that comes with a solid work ethic to not only get a job done, but to do it right.

One of Paul's greatest characteristics is that his immediate response to someone else's problem is to help them. He'll help his neighbor before he'll do his own work.

When it came to maintaining and remodeling the bank buildings, we quickly realized how efficient Paul could be which all came down to his common sense. He became a member of the board of directors for the Springville bank for that very reason.

Paul could do everything when it came to construction. He wasn't a guy who stood around and told a helper what to do. When it came to remodeling

207

teller windows, fixing up restrooms, pouring concrete for a parking lot, doing the electrical and plumbing, the heating and air conditioning, even changing light bulbs, Paul was doing the work.

Ernie Buresh (left) talks about renovation of Village Bank & Trust with Paul Nielsen as they renovated the bank to resemble its original look. (Photo courtesy of The Gazette.) Lower right, the room Paul built above the Buresh garage in Anamosa for Nan Wood Graham.

I had him finish some projects at home, too. In Anamosa, he raised the roof on our garage to put in a bedroom and a bathroom for the times Nan Wood Graham stayed with us. Many other friends stayed there as well, including one of Wendy's friends who lived with

us most of her senior year in high school.

As Paul worked on the remodeling, a couple of local contractors watched with interest to see what they could learn. It was amazing how Paul cut notches in the rafters, raised them, built the walls, then lowered the rafters again to fit perfectly into the notches.

Paul has such a mathematical brain, he can figure stuff out with ease. He's also meticulous in everything he does. It reminds me of the old Bohemian saying, "Dvakrat mer, jednou rez," which in English means, "Measure twice, cut once." That was a big thing with my mother. She used that saying in her rug weaving business a lot.

For me, Paul's crowning glory came when he built the Shueyville bank by himself. I designed it with Paul's oversight and then he went to work with those blueprints. He completed the new bank within a year and there were absolutely no change orders. I am just so amazed at how lucky I have been to find Paul. He built that bank as if it was his own.

Chapter 65

Friendship

with "An Old Shoe"

When a friendship lasts 60 years you know it's something special.

All of the relationships I was fortunate enough to enjoy were different in so many ways. That's what made them so valuable and one of those relationships is with Sandy Boyd.

He was a relatively new professor at the University of Iowa Law School when I was a student. I took business law from him and, since we were about the same age, we hit it off right away. Actually, the teacher was five months younger than the student. It seemed a little strange at first – you expect your teachers to be older than you – but that's why our relationship worked from the beginning.

I don't remember what grades I earned in Sandy's classes, but I'd be willing to bet they weren't A's. I never earned very many A's through my whole education.

After I graduated, though, our friendship continued. He was always in a good-natured mood. We'd go to parties and university gatherings. He'd always introduce me as the Mayor of Swisher.

Sandy Boyd, a 60-year friend of Ernie Buresh who was his law professor, became president of the University of Iowa.

It was my relationship with Sandy that began my relationship with the university. He's the one who made it possible for me to become a life trustee of the University of Iowa Foundation.

The way I see Sandy is that he's just an old shoe. You know what I mean by that. He was always so comfortable to be around. We could talk about anything – law, banking, current events, the university. Anything. Sandy had a way of talking to anyone about anything. He showed so much common sense, even early in our relationship, that he was sure to become successful no matter what he did and where he went.

From those early days, I don't think I could have predicted that Sandy would become president of the University of Iowa. He deserved it. He was a great president (1969 to 1981). He also deserved to be president at the Field Museum in Chicago which he did for 15 years after that.

I don't remember ever talking to Sandy about my decision to leave my short career as an attorney. I would have been too embarrassed. But, as I said, we talked about banking and other things.

For one of Sandy's birthdays in Chicago, his wife, Susan had a surprise party at the Field Museum.

Everything was all set up, all of his friends from Iowa were there and then Sandy walked into the room. He was floored, but he kept his composure. He'd been working on a presentation for the museum. He looked at all of us and said, "I've spent so much time on this speech, you're all going to have to listen to it." And he gave us that speech.

When Sandy was president at the university, we'd have lunch regularly. We'd always have the same thing – split pea soup. I got to where I liked it, too.

That's the way Sandy can bring you around. You might not know it until it happens, but then that's it. You like split pea soup. We also have one thing in common – we're both pack rats.

After Sandy returned to the University of Iowa, I went to visit him at his office at the Boyd Law Building. He wasn't there, but I'd never seen a more cluttered office in my life. I brought that up the next time we met.

Sandy just smiled. "I know," he said. "I've never met a paper I didn't like."

Chapter 66

University Relationships

It's not easy to develop true friendships with people who make the decisions for major businesses or corporations or even the University of Iowa. These people are always on guard. They know there are a lot of people who just want something from them. The world is full of brownnosers who are only fooling themselves because others see right through them.

My early friendship with Sandy Boyd, when he was a law school professor, started me on the path to forming so many wonderful relationships at the university for decades to come. It was because of Sandy that I became a life trustee of the University of Iowa Foundation more than forty years ago.

That brought me close to Darrell Wyrick, the first full-time employee of the foundation, who got the ball rolling. Today Lynette Marshall is the foundation president and she's simply amazing when it comes to organizing campaigns. She gets her plan ready and brings everybody together and says, "Ok, it's time for the big game. Here we go!"

Obviously, when you're on a board that's raising money for the university, you meet the president. It's kind of automatic because raising money is the president's full-time job or pretty close to that. So I've had the pleasure of being on a first-name basis with the presidents since I graduated from law school. The

213

first was Sandy, and after that were James O. Freedman, Hunter Rawlings, Mary Sue Coleman, David Skorton and now Sally Mason. I'm good friends with Dr. Jean Robillard, the vice president of medical affairs at the university, who is chairman of the committee to find the next president and is serving as interim president.

Once you get to know a few people, it snowballs if you let it, if you're honest about becoming friends. You stay in contact with people, but you don't want to become a pest. You know, it's like having company – after more than a few days it's like fish and things can start to smell. Unfortunately, too many people screw it up because they try too hard, they just can't quit brownnosing.

In the athletic department my first really good friend was Bump Elliott, the athletic director. Later Bump was on my bank board of directors. Joanne and I became close to Bump and his wife, Barb. We were going to football and basketball games so it wasn't hard to do once you met Bump – he's the most friendly, outgoing person. His accomplishments are ten feet long. Everybody likes Bump.

It was through Bump we became friends of Lute and Bobbi Olson, Hayden Fry, Tom Davis and Kirk and Mary Ferentz.

My daughter Sandy's times at University Hospitals, where she underwent tests and some procedures, brought us close to many of the doctors. Ken Goins was Sandy's doctor there. We got to know John Colloton, who really built the hospital into what it is today; I still regularly have lunch with him. I'm friends with Ken Kates, who is in charge of the hospital now, and Dr. Keith Carter, head of the ophthalmology department. I recently got to meet John Callaghan, the orthopedic surgeon who did my hip surgery, so I'll always remember him.

Everybody was amazingly good to Sandy when we'd go on the Presidents' Club tours. They were all first class. After Sandy died, Mary Sue Coleman and her husband, Ken, called from Michigan to offer their condolences, but they could hardly talk and had to call back later. Kirk and Mary Ferentz cut a trip short to come back for Sandy's memorial service.

The whole point is, use every opportunity you can to build relationships, a variety of relationships. You can help people out when they need you and they can help you out when you need them. Why would you ever pass that up?

The Bureshes joined the University of Iowa family that included John Colloton, retired administrator of University Hospitals, on a Presidents' Club cruise. From left to right are Joanne, Sandy, John Colloton and Ernie.

Chapter 67

Truckin' with Russ

I didn't know Russ Gerdin, the founder of Heartland Express trucking company out of North Liberty, that many years. But I never bonded with anyone faster than I did with Russ.

We were introduced to each other nine or ten years ago by Bill Bernau, one of my best law school friends. Bill was helping Russ with some reorganization at Hawkeye State Bank in Iowa City, which Russ owned. We talked business and hit it off right away.

"You scare the hell out of me," Russ said. "We think so much alike."

He laughed when he said it, but he said it several times early in our friendship so I know he meant it. But what did I know about trucking? You can haul a big load with a truck. That's about it.

I never had the feeling that I knew more about anything than anybody else. Everybody would scare me because I thought they were all a lot smarter.

Russ was very smart but he and I had a lot in common. He worked hard as a truck driver early in his career. We surrounded ourselves with good people. Like me, he would rather use pen and paper than a computer. And we believed that you don't buy something until you can truly afford it and retire the debt quickly.

As Russ grew Heartland Express into a huge company, he paid for his trucks as he went along.

Russ Gerdin, founder of Heartland Express trucking company, became a close friend to Ernie Buresh in a short time.

Russ had many interests different from mine, though. He liked to hunt and you can see evidence of that in the boardroom at Heartland Express. But, just to show how it's a small world, one of Russ' hunting buddies was Judge Larry Conmey of Anamosa, a good friend of mine.

Russ and I had a friendship that developed into one that included our wives – Joanne and Ann. Since Russ was also a believer in education and contributed to the University of Iowa, we followed the Hawkeyes and we both became friends of Kirk Ferentz, the head football coach, and his wife, Mary.

Some years back, Kirk called Joanne and asked if we would come to their house for dinner. The day we were invited happened to be after a spring game. He said the Gerdins were also invited and he would call Ann.

Since we didn't know where Kirk lived, we joined up with Russ and Ann for the trip. When we arrived, we sat in the car in the driveway for a couple of minutes. Before we knew it, Kirk came out wearing shorts and sandals. He was a lot more casually dressed than we were. After we chatted for a few minutes, Kirk asked if we wanted to come into the house. Russ said, "Sure," then looked at me and said, quietly, "I thought that's why we came."

We had quite a surprise when we went through the foyer and looked into the dining room. It was full of bedroom furniture. Russ turned to me and said, "It's a cinch we're not going to eat in here." Evidently the bedroom furniture was there while the room upstairs was being redone.

Mary, in a jean skirt and barefooted, greeted us in the kitchen and invited us to sit around the island counter. Kirk asked if we'd like a beer and we said, "Yes." We visited briefly and then Kirk picked up a package from the counter and left to the garage.

Russ turned to me again. "Geez," he said, "Do you think we have the wrong night?" I told him that was possible, that I hadn't taken the call but that Joanne had. He said he didn't take the call, either, that Ann did. So we were thinking the same thing.

Curiosity got the best of Russ, so we walked outside and found Kirk grilling steaks on the barbeque. We visited with him until the steaks were done and then, back in the house, Mary ushered us to a table set up on the screened-in porch. It turned out they'd been expecting us, they just didn't have the food out when we'd arrived.

Kirk and Mary prepared everything. We ate on the porch and it was one of the most enjoyable evenings of my life.

Russ and I would have lunch on occasion and we'd always talk on the phone. But he was a private person, too.

In 2006, I didn't know he was having a liver transplant until I was told about it at the Iowa-Iowa State football game. Since Russ was a big contributor to Iowa State, he was friends with President Greg

Geoffroy who approached me as we sat in Kinnick Stadium. "Do you know where Russ is now?" he asked. When I said no, he pointed to University Hospitals and said, "He's over there having a liver transplant."

Russ was the type of guy who'd do anything for you. After the Flood of 2008 in the New Bohemia area, I was at Village Bank when I saw a Heartland Express truck backed up to a house next door. The people who lived there were friends of Russ and Ann. The truck was there to move their belongings, what they could salvage.

When that truck pulled away, who do you think was driving? Russ Gerdin.

When Russ died in 2011, we lost a great friend. He had a number of different health problems and he didn't deserve any of them.

The Gerdins are perfect examples of the friends you like to have and that extends to their three children, too, because of the way they treat you and other people. They never give the impression that they're better than you or anyone else. Their success never interferes with the way they treat their friends.

You can include Kirk and Mary Ferentz in that group, too. These people are more interested in making friendships and developing relationships than in referring to their successes in any way.

Chapter 68

The Doctor is Always In

Every day that I stayed at Meth-Wick in Cedar Rapids for physical therapy in preparation for my hip surgery, Dr. Chirantan Ghosh stopped in to see me. He wanted to check my meds and to say hello.

When I told him he didn't need to do that, that he was busy enough with all of his patients at The Ghosh Center for Oncology and Hematology, do you know what he said? He said, "That's the way I practice medicine. I treat everybody the same."

Dr. Ghosh isn't even my primary doctor. But he's one of my best friends. And that's the kind of friend he is to all of his patients and to so many others.

I met the doctor at Village Bank in Cedar Rapids. He wanted to start his own business, Iowa Blood & Cancer Care. Dr. Ghosh had been with Oncology Associates in Cedar Rapids.

I guess Dr. Ghosh is from Kolkata, India, and since his first name begins with "C" and he was in Chicago and had other "Cs" in his life he wanted to end up in a town that began with "C," so he came to Cedar Rapids. Anyway, he had a heavy accent and I only understood about half of what he was telling me. But that was enough. I could tell how sincere he was and that he had great integrity. We gave him the loan he needed to start Iowa Blood & Cancer Care.

What I first admired about him was his business sense. So many doctors are not expected to have the best business judgment – when they're in medical school, medicine is what they study. They don't have time for business. But Dr. Ghosh had it. He would come in to borrow money for his chemotherapy drugs because they're very expensive and then the next week or so he'd pay off that loan after he was reimbursed by the insurance company.

As I got to know the doctor, there was so much more I liked about him. Everybody I talked to who was a patient of his had nothing but good things to say about his bedside manner, his compassion and his dedication to making them feel comfortable.

They say behind every good man is a good woman and Sima Ghosh is that woman. His wife is a big reason for his success and that of their children – they are truly a dedicated family. Not long ago we invited them to dinner with Gail Agrawal, the dean of the law school at the University of Iowa, and her husband, Dr. Naurang Agrawal, a clinical professor of internal medicine, who is from India. He and Dr. Ghosh did all of the talking so it was fascinating to just sit back and listen.

I really like how Dr. Ghosh wants to run the show, to make decisions. And he's good at it.

There are a lot of people who are afraid to make decisions, and that's too bad. They don't get anywhere. Then there are the people who always make bad decisions. They don't get anywhere, either.

Like Dr. Ghosh, I make my own decisions. I wouldn't have it any other way.

When my hip began hurting, Dr. Ghosh wanted to take charge. "Get it done. Get it done," he told me.

My hip didn't hurt that bad at first. He just kept prodding me. It really hurt by the time I had surgery. Listen to the doctor.

221

Chapter 69

60th Birthday

Letter from Wendy

When I turned 60, my older daughter's gift was a letter from her heart.

Wendy was 34 when she wrote it. I'd love to be 34 again, but that's not possible.

You can, however, reach out to the people you love at any age. You'll never do it any younger. And maybe those people, like me, will cherish your letter for the rest of their lives.

Here's Wendy's letter:

October 28, 1986
Dear Dad,

It seems to me that celebrating your sixtieth birthday calls for more than a pair of pajamas and a card. And since it also seems that there's way little I could buy you that you need or want, I'll try instead to put into words how I feel about you, as a person and as a father.

I can remember the "bear traps" you made to catch Sandy and me when we were little – and how you'd let us struggle and struggle and then finally get free. And I

222

remember my wonderful playhouse – that matched **our** *house – and even had a telephone that worked. You were so patient teaching me to ride my bike – and drive a car. You took us all over, too – and those trips every summer were more than just vacations; they solidified our sense of family and let us know each other better and away from our "home roles." Thank you for getting me a checking account in fourth grade – I felt very grown up and responsible, and I knew you had faith in me.*

It was harder for us when I hit puberty and cried a lot and wanted so hard to please you and never felt I did or was good enough. But that continual striving to achieve and please you certainly contributed to getting me through all my schooling. So, your contribution to that prolonged education was more than the sizeable financial outlay you made. Thank you.

We're better again at understanding each other as adults. You have been constantly supportive, both personally and professionally. And when I accomplished something, you shared my success as if it was your own.

You have accomplished so much. It amazes me to think of you running the feed store, building the house in Swisher, then going to law school, and buying banks. It's as if you've had more than one life – all of them different, each more productive and successful than the one life most of us live.

Your friends are good examples of this. You're comfortable with a great diversity of people – and they with you. I think you've had less recognition for all you've done than what you've deserved – perhaps out of jealousy, but perhaps you accomplish so much so seemingly effortlessly, and without doubt or negativism, that all you do is almost taken for granted, as if no one stops to think you put forth the time and work. The expectations of you are so high – and always met.

223

You are wonderful with your grandchildren, and they love you. You're always happy to see them and take some time for them. Katie may become a doctor, but I want T.J. to be a banker.

*There are lots of things that wouldn't have happened without you. And there are lots of things I wouldn't have done or been without you. The shape of my life today is inextricably tied to your influence. I am happy with it, and I thank you. Thank you for believing in me, supporting me (in **all** ways), standing by me, encouraging me.*

I love you very much.

Wendy

Retirement isn't an Option

ERNIE BURESH

Chapter 70

First Surgery at 88

Except for a tonsillectomy when I was young and cataracts later, my life was free of broken bones, serious illness and surgery. That is, until my left hip started bothering me to no end a few months before my 87th birthday.

Mowing the grass is one of my favorite getaways – I can ride the mower, concentrate on doing a good job and then feel a sense of accomplishment when I'm done. It probably goes back to the days when I mowed the lawn for the two widows in Western. But, in the summer of 2014, it was painful when I'd climb down off the tractor. I thought that's what caused my pain, the climb up and down.

One of the things about having a daughter who's a doctor is that she looks out for you. Wendy thought it might be more than sore muscles, so she insisted that I get a physical examination. In the end, it showed my hip bone had degenerated with age, that I had arthritis in my hip and some in my spine, and that my carotid artery was 70 to 75 percent blocked.

Wendy said I may be 88 years old but that, health-wise, I'm about 70. She knows. Some of her patients are the other way around – their health makes them seem older than their ages.

She knew how bad I wanted my hip repaired or replaced but wouldn't let me have that done until I had my carotid artery cleaned out. I probably wouldn't go to the doctor if it wasn't for Wendy. She's a blessing.

But, I'd be lying if I said having surgery didn't concern me. Someone asked if it scared me. I wouldn't say it scared me – I was terrified.

I barely remember the tonsillectomy when I was five or six years old, but I do know there was a lot of blood. You never forget something like that. I don't recall if I got ice cream afterward, and I love ice cream, but I remember the blood.

Medicine has come a long way since then. In my opinion, it's incredible. The instruments and the technology are fascinating, but it's really the doctors that are amazing. They're so well-trained and confident and you know they have excellent track records. Plus, a friend had his carotid artery unblocked a few weeks before I was to have mine done and he bounced right back.

You have that surgery to avoid having a stroke. That's a good thing. I've never had a problem with my heart and I stayed calm about it even the night before the surgery. It's simply a matter that you have to have it done if you want to live longer.

But I was still terrified. That doesn't go away, either. It's major surgery mainly because of the anesthesia you have to have for the surgery.

Joanne and Wendy were there with me. When I revived in the recovery room, I told them they could go home. I made it. You have to have faith in medicine – it's come so far in the last 20 – the last 50 – years.

I had to take it easy for six weeks. No shower for the first two weeks. Shaving was delicate with the big cut trying to heal on the right side of my neck. But it still didn't get rid of my pain. I needed my hip replaced.

After about three weeks, I started making arrangements at University Hospitals to have my hip done. At one of the interviews, a woman doctor said it's difficult to find a surgeon who wants to operate on an 88-year-old. I told her I couldn't go on living with this pain.

I was really going to be disappointed if the pain didn't go away or if I had another problem. My knee on the same side, on my left leg, hurts sometimes. I didn't want a whole new body. I just didn't want the pain.

February 2015

Dear Ernie & Joanne,
This is to wish you both a get well soon wish! Ernie, I knew about your 2 surgeries and I knew you are through the first with a new hip on the way — so my prayers continue to be with you. Joanne, I was so very sorry to learn that your flu had turned to pneumonia — so we are thinking of you both — a lot! Please get well soon and know how much we are thinking about you both! Warm regards,
Sally + Ken

We received this note from U of I President Sally Mason as I prepared to have two surgeries. It is included in this book to reveal the incredible character of a university president who takes time out of her unbelievably busy schedule to hand-write this note to a very ordinary couple who just like and appreciate Sally and Ken Mason and the University of Iowa.

Chapter 71

Observations:

Ernie's Tidbits

During the conversations I held with Ernie, in two-hour segments, one or the other of us would inevitably drift off-topic. It happens when you get along as well as we did, when one thought leads to another. Sometimes these extraneous stories would obviously become the start of a chapter for this book. Other times I'd jot down a note to file away for future reference in the event it fit in later.

Well, in the process of preparing and devouring all of the information, much like eating a huge Thanksgiving Day dinner, there are leftovers. While many of these morsels simply didn't fit in anywhere and wound up in the garbage, others were simply too tasty to ignore.

So here, in no particular order, are some of my favorite Ernie tidbits:

"I'm at the stage in my life where I don't believe anything I hear and I only believe about half of what I see." (At 88 years old, Ernie, you're entitled.)

"In my opinion . . ." (Ernie often started his explanation of the way he sees something with this phrase.)

"Every mistake, every failure, is a learning experience."

"Criticism is negative. There ought to be a way to do it in a positive way."

"It amazes me how many cars don't have left turn signals." (Like many of us, Ernie is frustrated that so many people don't use their turn indicators, to which he adds, "Don't get me started on other drivers.")

Ernie Buresh poses with Queen, a dog he had while growing up.

"Everybody should have a dog. I'm a big dog lover. Cats are OK, too. When you're growing up, everybody should have a dog, a pet. It teaches responsibility." (Dogs also provide love and a welcome connection to the past as shown by Mattie, the 14-year-old Shih Tzu that had been daughter Sandy's trusted companion before she died.)

"Many of my friends consider themselves to be middle class. Actually, they're first class when it comes to character, friendliness and compassion."

"I'm not a big fan of tipping, but I do it. Howard Hall was a great tipper – everybody wanted to wait on his table. But the whole thing about tipping is confusing. Who do you tip? I've had wonderful employees at my

233

banks through the years. They would sit down with customers for two hours to help reconcile their accounts. We never charged for that, but other banks did. Anyway, I never heard from even one employee that they received a tip for this extra service, yet they deserved it as much as anyone."

"One thing that's important in life is recognizing considerate and thoughtful people. Thoughtfulness is a real asset."

"When I hired employees for my community banks, I had a preference for people from smaller communities. They seemed to be more friendly and had a really good work ethic and required less (oversight)."

"It's hard to fire somebody but in some cases it has to be done. I had to fire a guy once because he got his hand caught in the till." (Howard Hall had a policy of never hiring back someone who had been fired, which brings to mind the popular business management philosophy: "It's not the people you fire who cause you problems, it's the people you don't fire.")

"Treat everybody fair and you won't get into trouble. But, no matter how hard you try to be fair, you tend to give easy assignments to people who aren't as competent as others and you lean on those who have the talent and drive to succeed."

"You want to find someone who is confident, but not so confident that they go ahead and do something on their own that doesn't turn out as they expected so it screws everybody else up. I had that once. A guy I totally relied on stretched the truth. Half of the things he said weren't true. I couldn't trust him."

"I do not like brownnosers. I can spot them a mile away. People ruin themselves – and I don't understand why they can't see it – by being brownnosers."

"Likes are positives. Dislikes are negatives. Life is all about positives. Forget about negatives. They're no good."

"All of my life I didn't think I had any particular talents or anything positive about my appearance. Some people can use their good looks to get ahead, but that only goes so far. I never had that advantage."

"The more I look at what some businesses spend on unnecessary things, the more I get discouraged. They're expenses these people should realize affect their bottom line. It's also a way to evaluate their ability to change; their management ability. If I've got an expense that's eating me up, every night I go to bed I look for ways to minimize it. At least recognizing excessive spending is a form of success."

"So many of my friends are dying. When somebody dies, I call the family to express my condolences, to let them know how much that person meant to me. So many people don't do this. The family always thanks me. They appreciate it."

"I don't know that I was good. I know that I was lucky."

Dave Rasdal

Chapter 72

The Banks are Robbed

Of course you worry about bank robberies, but you can't dwell on them. It doesn't do any good. You can put every possible security measure in place, but you can never predict when someone might try to rob your bank. When it happens, be ready.

During my 52 years in the business, we had three bank robberies and one embezzlement. The embezzlement was such a little deal we let the person go and didn't pursue it legally.

The Shueyville bank was kind of an inside job; the two robberies at Village Bank and Trust in Cedar Rapids were typical – a guy in disguise passed a note, he was given money, he ran and the police caught him.

The first Village Bank robbery occurred at the original building at Third Street and Twelfth Avenue SE. One of my employees chased the robber and when the police arrived they arrested him under the Sixteenth Avenue Bridge. The second one was in January after the Floods of 2008 when we'd closed the old bank and opened an office in a medical building at Second Avenue and Tenth Street SE. The police caught that robber a few days later.

The Shueyville bank robbery in the summer of 2002 was a scary ordeal, especially for our employee, Stacy Christner. She was a model employee and would sometimes go to work early.

When Stacy did that one day, she opened the door and was grabbed from behind by a man with a gun. She did all the right things – she didn't fight, she gave him the money and she didn't get hurt.

The sad thing is that Stacy resigned, knowing that she couldn't work in a bank anymore for fear of another robbery.

The robber in this case took a good sum of money and escaped in Stacy's car. Since it took several years to catch him, we lost the money, although our insurance covered it minus the deductible.

When I first started in the banking business, back in the 1950s, Merchants National Bank in Cedar Rapids always had a guard on duty. I never had a guard in any of my banks. When cameras came along, they became a great deterrent.

I always thought it would be clever to have a trap door in front of the teller. You'd hit a button under the counter and drop the robber into the basement. I could have had a trap door installed when we built the Shueyville bank, but any robber who came in probably would have gone to the other window.

The sign still welcomes visitors to Shueyville, even though the Exchange State Bank is no longer open.

Chapter 73

Moving on from Banking

I was always in the market to buy bank stock, not sell it. That was a bad habit of mine. It's always fun to buy.

In 1983, though, a Cedar Rapids businessman approached me about buying controlling interest in City National Bank which had assets of about $22 million. At the time selling it made sense. Howard Hall founded City National in 1957 and I had been on its board since 1968, but it was a Cedar Rapids bank. The other banks were in rural Iowa which was much more familiar to me, having grown up poor in Western and Shueyville when I barely knew what a bank was. It's a matter of how everything fits into what you're trying to do which was to help people who came from similar situations. So, we sold that bank.

A few years later, after Joanne and I moved to Cedar Rapids, we thought it would be a good idea to sell the Anamosa bank. That also included a branch office in Tipton.

We kept the other banks for almost another 20 years and in 2003 opened Village Bank at Third Street and Twelfth Avenue SE in the New Bohemia area of Cedar Rapids. That was kind of like going home – the area was so familiar to me because we visited it often when I was a youngster. And it was a beautiful old bank building that we completely remodeled.

238

Then the flood hit in 2008. I realized it was time for me to bail out. The flood destroyed Village Bank. Guy Sleep, my right-hand-man, had retired. I had to consider that I was past 80 years old and still trying to do what I'd been doing 30 years ago. Age and energy level were certainly deciding factors. So we found buyers for each bank and the Village Bank building.

I always approached management of the banks on the theory that they don't run themselves, even though some people think they do. You have to put in a lot of attention and effort if you're going to be hands-on no matter what you do. You rely on people like Guy Sleep and everything changes when they retire.

When you like to buy, sure it's hard to sell. It's also hard because I'd been in the business for 52 years. I'd never say I had a favorite bank – they each presented their own benefits and challenges – but I'd be lying if the Martelle bank wasn't close to my heart since it was the first one. Also, I'm disappointed that the Exchange State Bank near Shueyville isn't still operating. We worked hard to get it going from scratch and I was proud to serve the area I'd known in childhood. I guess the new owners decided it wasn't big enough so they closed it.

To me, it all boils down to this – if you don't exert enough effort to make anything you do work, then it's not going to work.

I miss banking. On the other hand, it's not the same. Rules and competition have changed. So, in a way, I'm glad I'm not involved. But, I'm still busy. There's no way I consider myself retired.

Chapter 74

Married 65 Years

Joanne and I were married in 1949, on November 24, at the Little Brown Church. It's so long ago I hardly remember it. When you think back, it was kind of the road to survival. You got married, you spent time together, you had kids. It was just natural. I've never really thought about it any other way.

There's not really a secret to being married for 65 years. I'll tell people we're not really compatible, but that's supposed to be a joke. What we are is committed.

We made a commitment to each other and from my standpoint our commitment changed. I think Sandy's illness – I'm positive of it – had a big impact on 65 years. We were committed to her and each other and everything else.

One place where Joanne excelled is that she's a really good cook and a good housekeeper. That's important to me. I like everything organized and clean.

Joanne is German and I'm Czech. Each of the languages, on their own, can be difficult to pronounce but, in my opinion, there are a lot of similarities in the food. I learned that early on living not far from the Amana Colonies. If you ask Joanne about her cooking, she loves to tell how I went from 155 pounds to 175 pounds that first year we were married. I loved everything she fixed and that included two pies a week just for the two of us.

The first month of our married life we lived in a motel room in Ames. Joanne fixed food on a hotplate. We'd even set up a card table and entertained guests. Then it was on to the one-bedroom walkup in Marshalltown for a year and 11 years in Swisher. That's when we became a family. Life just took over.

Ernie and Joanne Buresh pose for their 50th wedding anniversary portrait.

I think realizing that your likes and dislikes are compatible is important. Our interests over the years changed and developed. We used to go to Chicago for a weekend and leave the girls home. For our 25th anniversary we had dinner with friends at the Drake. But, for our 50th anniversary, we took the family, the

241

kids and the grandkids, to Disneyworld in Orlando and went on a Disney cruise. That's the year Wendy put our picture in the paper and I didn't really want that. Nobody cares if you're married 10 minutes or 10 years.

Our habits contributed to the life we've had. We never put ourselves into positions where we had any problems with our finances or our health. Neither one of us smoke or drink. But we played cards – 500 and bridge. We were fine being partners but we were good competitors, too. Joanne likes to read and I can spend that time going over my books. On television she likes movies, I like the news and we will watch Wheel of Fortune together.

Sometimes I think how lucky we are. From my standpoint, our commitment was almost totally to Sandy. With Wendy, sometimes that wasn't easy, but we were fortunate she was smart and a great sister. I'll give Wendy a lot of credit and all of the credit to Joanne.

Joanne was a saint with Sandy. Sometimes I know she thought she was neglecting me but I never felt that way. We brought Sandy into the world and we took care of her together. More than anything else, it was the commitment and compassion we both had with Sandy. And as we got older, Sandy did more and more for us because I think she was worried how our lives had changed.

Joanne is always trying to do too much. All through the ordeal with my hip surgery, she was there every minute. I worried about it. She's 84. When I was recovering at University Hospitals she was there for two nights. She was taking care of Hilltop which is a big house. When you're in your 80s this is a huge concern. She's doing too much but she won't listen to me.

When I came back to my room at Meth-Wick for recovery the doctors and therapists were worried that I wasn't eating. The food is good, it's just not what I'm used to, do you know what I mean? Joanne went out and got me a fast-food roast beef sandwich and I ate the whole thing. She brought me some of her homemade three-bean salad and I ate all of that.

Joanne knows what I need. That's what marriage is all about.

Chapter 75

Have Children, Will Travel

My mother enjoyed traveling. She and my father drove all the way from Iowa to Yellowstone National Park in the 1920s when that was really a journey. They didn't have much money, but they knew the unbelievable value of visiting other parts of the country. My mother was still traveling into her 80s. I probably got my enjoyment of seeing the world from her.

More than that, though, were better opportunities with improved roads and advancements in flying. And, having children. Everybody can learn a lot by exploring new places, but it's best for the children.

When I was growing up in Western and couldn't even afford to put 19-cent-a-gallon gas in my car, I never in my wildest dreams thought I'd have the opportunity to see Czechoslovakia. To see where your people came from, your ancestors, gives you a sense of pride that you can't get any other way. Do it without hesitation.

With regards to my family, I remember we took our station wagon all the way to New York in 1964 for the World's Fair. We enjoyed it so much we went back again the next year. I drove in all that traffic, through the Lincoln Tunnel and found parking. I'd never do that today. But, if you turned the clock back 50 years, I'd do it all over again.

I'd say my favorite family trip was to New Zealand and Australia. The prime minister of New Zealand had a connection to Cornell College in Mount Vernon, so he gave us suggestions. We set up a wonderful tour by minivan, so use connections when you can. We also went south for a once-in-a-lifetime visit to Phillip Island to see the penguins.

The huge globe at the New York World's Fair serves as a backdrop for Joanne Buresh and her daughters, Wendy (center) and Sandy, on their visit in 1964.

Whenever we traveled, Sandy loved to buy postcards for the pictures, then write them out and send them to friends back home. She was our chief correspondent. She loved to receive mail and she knew other people are the same way.

Joanne would slip the extra postcards Sandy bought as souvenirs into our suitcase and we'd bring them home. We still have stacks of those postcards from Sandy.

Chapter 76

The Death of a Child

We think about Sandy every minute of every day. She is always in our minds and she died more than three years ago. But she will always be with us. Unless you lose a child, you have no idea how it is.

When I think about our daughter, I think about all of the other people who have children that need special attention. There are more parents out there like that than you think.

The Buresh family used this picture on a Christmas card a couple of years before Sandy died. From left to right are Sandy, Wendy, Joanne, Ernie and Sandy's dog, Mattie.

Having grown up poor, I also think of the poor people who can't afford to give their children the proper health care. Life becomes even more difficult for them. They have so many more worries. You never know when you might get sick, when your child may need special medical attention. Having affordable health coverage is extremely important.

We were lucky in that respect when Sandy was born in 1954 and had her first surgery five years later. By then I had health coverage at Merchants National Bank. It would have been very difficult for us without that.

More than anything, though, I have to point to Joanne. She was a saint with our daughter. Joanne gave Sandy all of the care she could. Joanne did more than anybody could have expected her to do for Sandy. More than just being a mother, Joanne was Sandy's best friend.

When you have a child who needs special attention, it takes much, much, much more effort than you can imagine. First, give them the love they need. Second, give them the help they need.

I tried to treat Sandy like any other child so I denied her some of the things she wanted to do. They were little things, but they were important to her at the time. I was ignorant and just didn't think about it. I'll never live down that regret. No matter how much you try to do for someone to make up for your mistakes, you can never do enough.

Sandy was a forgiving person. She wanted everybody to be her friend and to visit with her. That wasn't always going to happen as she pictured it, so she suffered mentally. She had physical and mental pain and suffering. We did as much as we could at the time for her physical needs. And Sandy never complained. I never heard her complain. She just took everything in stride.

Except for her heart procedures and repairing her paralyzed palate when she was young, Sandy went through most of her life with only minor surgeries. The only other major surgery Sandy had was a cornea transplant for her keratoconus at University Hospitals in Iowa City in the 1990s.

That was about the time Wendy thought Prozac might help Sandy better cope with her life. She was very self-conscious and often thought other people were looking at her because she was different, even though her appearance was like that of any young adult as she grew up. After a doctor prescribed Prozac for Sandy, her fears disappeared. It made all the difference in the world when she was out in public, when we went on trips, when Joanne took her on visits back to Anamosa.

Sandy Buresh shares lunch with her grandmother, Emma Buresh, in 1995.

My advice is, if you have a youngster who needs special attention, you have to take a lot of time to figure out what you can do to make life better and easier for them. You don't want to have regrets. But it's not easy.

Someone suggested that having a dog would help Sandy. I'm a dog lover so it made sense to me. We contacted the Cedar Valley Humane Society about that and the day they called we went out to look at this dog. Mattie is a Shih Tzu. She's such a charmer. Sandy fell in love with her from that first moment. They slept together from that first night on.

Mattie as she looked in 2002 about the time she became Sandy Buresh's constant companion.

After Sandy died, Mattie kept running up to Sandy's room to find her. It was sad. It took Mattie a long time to get used to Sandy being gone. To this day Mattie doesn't want Joanne or me to leave her. She's afraid the same thing will happen.

About the time of Sandy's fifty-seventh birthday in October, 2011, some health problems that had always seemed minor became worse. Her ankles and feet swelled from water retention. She had a loss of energy.

Joanne kept up with the regular activities that included getting her hair done and visiting friends in Anamosa. That seemed to pick her up. But then other things frustrated her. She seemed physically weaker. She had more and more trouble getting in and out of the bathtub.

Early in 2012, even though Sandy was feeling down, I talked her into going on one of our regular trips to Kalona. She picked out a novelty item at the Kalona Country store as usual, but had to sit down and rest, which wasn't normal. We ate at the Family Restaurant, one of her favorites, but she seemed lethargic and didn't eat much. She was too tired to visit the bakery or to stop at the casino in Riverside where she had always liked to play the slot machines for a few minutes. She just wanted to go home.

Sandy's heart was failing. We took her to St. Luke's Hospital in Cedar Rapids but doctors said there wasn't anything they could do. We took her home and had health care for her there.

The day before Sandy died, she looked up at me with those sad eyes. She said, "Dad, I don't think I'm going to make it."

As a parent, you don't want to believe that when you hear it from your own child. You have a strong sense of denial. You always think you'll outlive your children.

The next day Sandy looked at me again in that same way. Her voice was weaker this time. "Dad," she said. "I'm dying."

Sandy died that day, Feb. 22, 2012. She was 57.

After Sandy died, so many people called. One of them was Mary Sue Coleman, former president of the University of Iowa, who was president at the University of Michigan. She got to know Sandy on the presidential tours and they became pals.

When Mary Sue Coleman called from Michigan to tell us how sorry she was, she got all choked up and couldn't talk. She handed the phone to her husband, Ken, who is originally from Marion, and he admitted he wasn't much better off. He choked up, too. They had to hang up. Ken said they'd call back later and they did.

Mary Sue Coleman, then president of the University of Iowa, with Sandy and Joanne Buresh.

Since Sandy died, Joanne and I try to visit her crypt a couple of times a week at Cedar Memorial Park in Cedar Rapids. We change the flowers there once a week.

In my mind I see Sandy every day so I feel so much better going there because I feel closer to her. I don't know of anything else I can do. I miss her.

Chapter 77

University

Relationships Continue

The University of Iowa has become such a big part of our lives now that it kind of dwarfs the growing up poor part of my life. It is something I cherish so much, though, because it constantly reminds me of how lucky I've been.

It has been sad to see that Sally Mason is retiring as president of the university. If you know Sally Mason, there's something different about her, in a good way.

Ernie Buresh is flanked by Sally Mason, (left) and Lynette Marshall at a recent University of Iowa Foundation function.

Sally Mason amazes me because she's so knowledgeable about anything. She's been under fire a lot and for what reason? She has handled it really well. She had the flood in 2008 and other controversies. We talked about her retiring. When she told me her decision, she said it was time and that she felt good about how things were going to work out like we'd talked about. I'm happy she'll still have some involvement with the university.

Sally Mason delivered the eulogy at Sandy's memorial service. Lynette Marshall, president of the university foundation, also gave a eulogy. The entire university and the foundation were so good to Sandy.

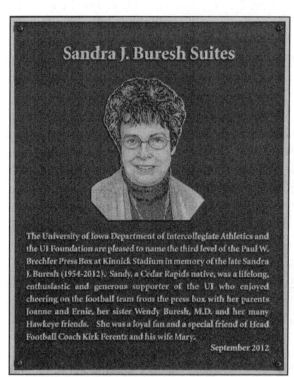

The University of Iowa athletic department dedicated the third level of the press box at Kinnick Stadium to Sandy Buresh in the fall of 2012.

Gary Barta, the athletic director at the University of Iowa, and Andy Piro, an assistant athletic director, were behind having the third floor at Kinnick Stadium named after her – the Sandra J. Buresh Suites. They're putting together a collage there and one of the pictures shows Sandy eating a hotdog at a football game. It was taken by Governor Bob Ray who was always an avid photographer.

Ernie Buresh, left, chats with former Iowa Governor Bob Ray in a suite at Kinnick Stadium in Iowa City during a Hawkeye football game in 1994.

Bob Ray and his wife, Billie, and family were regular guests of ours for football games and his daughters, especially Lu Ann, were really good to Sandy. We

255

visited the Rays at Terrace Hill in Des Moines when he was governor and I still talk to them regularly. That just shows how relationships build on each other; how they are so important.

Whenever the law school had a function, a dinner or event, Dean N. William Hines always included Sandy. He personally made sure she had a Coke and whatever else she needed.

Dave Dierks, who has been with the University foundation more than 40 years, almost as long as I've been a board member, was always the instigator to make sure Sandy was included in their events. Dave is the type of person who likes to take you to lunch. He tells you all about what's going on. He loves to talk, but he's a great listener, too. If you need something done through the foundation you can count on him. He's semi-retired but still travels around the country to talk to donors. He's so busy, yet he still finds time to call me to see how I'm doing.

As a poor kid growing up in Shueyville, Iowa, and even as a law school student, I could never have imagined that the University of Iowa would become such a huge part of our lives, that the relationships we developed so many years ago and through the years would mean so much to me today.

You can never make too many friends and you never know what new friendships might develop from knowing those people – it is truly amazing and endless.

Chapter 78

Preserving Czech Heritage

Being a Czech who has lived in and around Cedar Rapids my entire life, I was more than happy to become a part of preserving that past in Cedar Rapids. After all, growing up in Western, south of Cedar Rapids, during the 1930s, we frequently made trips to the Sixteenth Avenue business district and the New Bohemia area on the other side of the river.

As I've mentioned before, since we were poor, our shopping trips were to buy only necessities. We stopped at the grocery store and dropped off the milk

and eggs from the farm and the rugs my mother made. If I had a quarter burning a hole in my pocket from mowing the widows' lawn, I'd buy a nickel ice cream cone at Old Mill Ice Cream on Third Street SE.

The National Czech & Slovak Museum & Library clock tower in Cedar Rapids was a gift from the Ernie Buresh and Les Buresh families.

257

Even though this wasn't in the Czech area, I laugh when I remember the Cedar Rapids Store owned by Jack Yeager where farmers bought overalls. He had been at street level, but moved his store to the second floor. He used the advertising slogan, "We moved upstairs to keep prices down."

The music system for the clock tower at the National Czech & Slovak Museum & Library was donated by Sandy Buresh in memory of her longtime friend Nan Wood Graham.

When the Czech Fine Arts Foundation decided to build a new museum, my brother, Les, and I decided we wanted to do something special. We set up a bank account for our donations. When the time came to look at the design for the new building we liked the idea of a clock tower right in front and donated enough money to have it built. That clock tower was inspired by the clock tower at the end of the Charles Bridge in Prague. Later, when Sandy inherited some money from Nan Wood Graham, she used that to purchase the carillon music for the tower.

The Flood in 2008 was disappointing – all of the destruction in Cedar Rapids and especially at the National Czech & Slovak Museum & Library. Not long before that I'd purchased the last original house remaining on Sixteenth Avenue to donate to the museum. I was amazed at how the property hadn't been maintained – the people must not have had money to keep it up. So Paul Nielsen went in for me and did all of the repairs before we gave the house to the museum in honor of my mother as the Babi Buresh Center. The house was damaged in the flood, too, but at least they were able to save it and fix it up again.

The Babi Buresh Center, donated to the Czech museum by Ernie Buresh in memory of his mother, Emma Buresh, was damaged in the Flood of 2008 but later repaired by the museum. (Photo courtesy of The Gazette.)

I am glad the clock tower was saved, too, but it almost seems out of place now so far from the museum. In my opinion, they should have kept the old museum building where it was instead of moving it up on the hill. I thought they could have renovated it and used it as an entertainment hall and just cleaned it out if it flooded again. But the people in charge told me FEMA wouldn't allow that. It didn't matter what I thought.

That reminds me of the time I was able to look at the plans for the museum before it was built. When I pointed out there were no electrical outlets in the library, they put in a change order to have more outlets added at a cost of $2,500. In my opinion, they also needed more of a reception area inside rather than having people just come into the grand hall. I thought having a terrazzo flood didn't make sense in a museum so it didn't surprise me when they added carpet to keep noise down. But, I tell you, what really puzzled me was the men's restroom that didn't have a urinal. It must be the only museum in the world without a urinal in the men's room.

There's no question the National Czech & Slovak Museum & Library is a beautiful place. It brings a lot of people to Iowa and to Cedar Rapids. I am proud to be Czech and to have been a small part of it.

Chapter 79

Ethics and the Truth

Too many people have a tendency to think you can ignore conflicts and ethics. You can't. Everybody needs to realize how important ethics are.

The survival and success of a bank, to a great extent, is a result of the integrity of its customers. When they say they're going to pay a loan back and they do, that's integrity. They demonstrate their own code of ethics. Those are the customers you want. Those are the type of people you want to surround yourself with.

Ethics and the absence of conflict were always important points I made to my bank directors. You need to always be above board. We had a zero tolerance for conflicts that affected the smooth operation of business. Any breach of ethics could be even worse.

There was also no room for schmoozers, brownnosers, people who act really nice to get what they want. What bothers me along the same line is when people don't tell the truth. That's one of the biggest things you have to deal with and it's almost impossible to detect sometimes. More and more people, it seems, have a tendency to not tell the truth over the littlest things. So many times there's really no reason for it. To some people it becomes a habit. I don't understand it.

Another thing that has always bothered me is how some people use a board membership to advance their own personal agendas. Sometimes it seems that's the only reason they're on the board. I've seen that happen more than once. To me that's not ethical.

If you can't tell the truth, then just don't say anything. If you have questionable ethics be prepared to defend yourself if that's even possible. The solution is really quite simple. Use common sense. Be the kind of person you, yourself, would want to have as a friend and business associate.

Chapter 80

To Sell the Farm

One minute it seems like we bought the farm just yesterday and the next minute I can't believe it's been in the family for 60 years. I know we can't own the farm forever, so it's time to think about selling it. But, when you think about what all it has meant through the years, that's not an easy move to make.

As much as anything, the farm represents my efforts to leave my poor childhood behind. Yet, it's also a way for me to remain connected to that part of my life since it's in Shueyville, so close to where I grew up.

Does that make sense? It does to me.

Many, many times I've been lucky in my life. But buying the 118-acre farm for $10,000 and selling 11 acres of it for $11,000 a year later to the Iowa Department of Transportation stands out. It has been free and clear since.

I've always been able to rent the farm ground, even though the price per acre has fluctuated with the economy. My tenants today are the best I've ever had.

The house that was on the property has been rented to the same tenants for 40 years. It started as a husband and wife with their daughter and now it is just the daughter. Since her father died and her mother is in a care center, I reduced the rent. You want to keep your long-term tenants happy.

I built a house for my parents' retirement years on the farm. We used some old brick from the old creamery we tore down on the Anamosa property where the library building stands. The house was sold years ago after my father died and when my mother moved to The Meth-Wick Community in Cedar Rapids.

The Shueyville bank building is still part of the farm. The bank isn't operating, but it would be a good location for some business since it's close to Interstate 380. In all, we've got 101 acres of the farm left. That's what could be sold.

In recent years I've had sales people approach me about selling the farm, but that's something I will arrange myself. I've never really thought about selling it until now. It will have to be done sooner rather than later, but it's not easy to let go of something that's been such an important part of you for your entire adult life.

Chapter 81

500 Friends

A favorite way to make and keep friends has always been to gather around a card table. Two Army buddies – Don Grovert of Newhall and Glen Dietrich of Van Horne – and I enjoyed playing 500. It wasn't long after World War II that we included our wives and it just grew from there.

As hard as it may seem in this day and age, we played for 50 years. It didn't matter if there was a snow storm or if it was raining hard with thunder. We never missed a month. Sometimes we'd play twice in a month. But, rain or shine, we always had our 500 party.

Usually a dozen of us would get together for dinner at one couple's house and follow it up with cards. In addition to Don and Joan Grovert and Glen and Lois Dietrich, at various times we were joined by Al and Lola Maye Krug of Newhall, Leonard and Georgina Mouchka of Amana, Don and June Krebs of Cedar Rapids, Lloyd and Leona Barry of Newhall and Alden and Corleen Morrison of Newhall.

The great thing about playing 500 was that it's complicated enough that you need to pay attention if you want to win, but it's not so complicated that you can't talk about other things while you're playing. Of course, it was never about winning. It was about fun. Every night was enjoyable. It was about spending time with friends, keeping up with their lives and sharing what had been going on in yours.

The 500 card club that met for 50 years poses for a picture at the Buresh home in Anamosa at Christmas, 1973. Front row, left to right, are Joanne Buresh, Lois Dietrich and Leona Barry. In the second row are Don Grovert, Al Krug, Leonard Mouchka, and Glen Dietrich. In back are Ernie Buresh, Lloyd Barry, Georgina Mouchka, Lola Maye Krug and Joan Grovert.

In the early days we played well into the night, but as we all got older we'd quit sooner and sooner each night. Joanne and I often hosted on New Year's Eve in Anamosa.

If I remember right, our last gathering was on New Year's Eve at Hilltop, our home in Cedar Rapids. As we talked about playing the next year it became obvious that age had caught up with us. We'd have to use more and more substitutes. Some of the people had health problems and others had died. We had a great run with great friends. We played 500 for 50 years.

Chapter 82

Nurturing

Personal Relationships

My mother had more influence on my life than anybody else and I tried to remember that every minute she was alive. The only thing she ever expected of me was that I'd grow up to be somebody she could be proud of. It doesn't cost one cent to give of yourself or to become the type of person other people hope you'll become. You could call it conscientious integrity.

MOTHER MINE
The world is full of mothers
Who are sweet and true,
But none of them can be
Half as wonderful as you.

A card recently discovered in a picture frame that Ernie Buresh may have given his mother when he was a child.

So many other personal relationships define who you become. These aren't the ones that necessarily come by doing business with somebody or even the ones that you develop when you connect with, say, your doctor's office or a large institution like the

University of Iowa. In this regard, I truly believe that a generous person is one who helps somebody out when that somebody can do nothing for them in return.

When I think of this, Joanne's father, George Paulsen, tops my list of personal relationships. We wouldn't have had anywhere near the life we've had without his influence. I'm going well beyond the $1,000 he gave us not to have a big wedding. He was so willing to help us out in so many ways and he had so many connections who would do the same. He was a lot more than just my father-in-law.

The difference between George and my father was black and white. My father's reputation didn't help us at all, but it didn't hurt us either. Joanne's dad's reputation did nothing but help us. That we ended up in Jones County was just a coincidence, nothing more.

As I said before, early in our marriage we'd visit Joanne's parents in Onslow nearly every weekend to do laundry, and they'd always send us home with plenty of food. My mother did the same when we'd visit them – give us eggs and chickens. I tried to do everything I could to pay them back, but it's one of those things you can never do. And the great thing about it is that they don't expect you to. They never even considered getting something in return for their favors.

At the Paulsen's I'd do all the odd jobs I could find – their house was built in 1936, so I painted and caulked and even fixed some electrical wiring once. Pretty soon they had honey-do lists for me. It made me feel good to contribute to their household, as I'm sure they felt about contributing to ours. It was simply what you did for each other.

Some business relationships naturally turn into personal relationships and none more so for me than my friendship with Howard Hall. At the bank and sometimes at our meetings at Brucemore, we were more about business than friendships. But weekends, when we'd go to Iowa football games or visit at their Palisades cottage, it was all about being friends. Since we both grew up in small towns I think it was easy for us to see the difference between business and true friendship.

So many other relationships I've had seemed to be more on a personal level than professional – especially with my brother, Les. He was always my brother first. We both worked hard to remember that. Money is far less important than friendship even within the family.

I could name so many other people, but I think about Sandy Boyd at the University of Iowa. He was my teacher in law school but after I graduated – even before that – our relationship was personal. When people learned I was friends with Sandy Boyd it was amazing. Doors seemed to open by magic.

Dave Dierks, a staff member at the University of Iowa Foundation, has been a trusted friend to Ernie Buresh for more than 40 years.

One of those doors was to the personal relationship I developed with Dave Dierks, who came to the University of Iowa Foundation as the director of planned giving about the time I became a board member. After Dave met our family, he took Sandy under his wing. He liked how Sandy was always upbeat, always cheering for the Hawkeyes even when they didn't have a chance to win.

Dave has spent his whole career traveling around Iowa and the country developing relationships. That was a major connecting point for us. We both believe some relationships are destined to be short-term and others are meant to last a lifetime, but they are all so very important.

Personal relationships are all about spending time together. Time doesn't cost you anything out of your pocket but it's impossible to put a value on relationships.

Cherish them. Nurture them. Pass them on.

Chapter 83

Good Samaritans

The world is full of Good Samaritans and a lot of the time that's your neighbors. It's a shame when you hear how neighborhoods have changed and people who live right next door to each other don't even become friends. The more friends you have, the more relationships you can build, the better off everybody becomes. I think that's what neighbor means.

In Anamosa, people all around our house befriended us from the day we moved in.

Esther and Joe Legg, across the street, became good friends immediately. Both Wendy and Sandy really enjoyed Esther, who was a 4-H leader. She took Sandy to church choir practice on Wednesdays because she knew Sandy would enjoy it. Esther was in the choir. The Leggs have a son who is deaf, so they know what it's like to have a child who needs special attention.

Eli and Rosalie Shada went quickly from acquaintances to friends in Anamosa, too. I had breakfast with Eli most every morning for many years. Joanne didn't drink coffee before we moved to Anamosa, but pretty soon she had joined Rosalie's backyard coffee club.

Coffee clubs were great places to make friends and they were often your neighbors, too. Joanne would take Sandy to the Casual Café and after that closed they'd go to Tucker's Tavern in the afternoons for the coffee club.

Ernie Buresh pushes good friend Eli Shada in a wheelbarrow down Anamosa's Main Street during a Ridiculous Days parade early in Ernie's life in Anamosa.

We fondly remember Martha Switzer who died of bone cancer. She was a few years older than Sandy, but she'd take her on casual drives just so they could enjoy the scenery and each other's company. They'd often drive through Wapsipinicon State Park where they'd look at nature and the flowers and wade across the shallow upside down bridge. That was a favorite thing for Sandy.

Dr. John Bailey used to be our neighbor before he moved to a new home overlooking the park at the southwest edge of Anamosa. As a friend, he went with me to Chicago to pick up Sandy from the hospital after her second heart surgery there. She was 10 years old and had a fever. The hospital didn't want to release her unless a doctor was present. John did this for us even though it was his wife's birthday. They both made a sacrifice.

Eleanor and Jack Schmidt lived close by and were great neighbors and friends to us and Sandy. Whenever we'd leave, they'd dog-sit Mattie. You know how much Sandy thought of them because she absolutely loved her dog.

Even now at Hilltop, it's hard to imagine life without neighbor friends. Larry Heald has rented the house to the north for a dozen years. He brings us the mail every day but does more than that, too. He plows the snow off the driveway in the winter and since I can't mow any more, he's taken it upon himself to mow the entire yard.

After my hip surgery when I needed a haircut and couldn't easily get out of the house, Marsha Stickle came over and cut my hair. Marsha and Rick Stickle have been terrific. She's cut my hair several times since that time and doesn't charge for it. Rick checks on my bank building in Shueyville to make sure it's OK and that the lights aren't on when they don't need to be so that we don't waste electricity. We let people use the bank lot to park cars when they're carpooling along I-380 because I think that helps security, too.

Through the years, we've enjoyed being friends with these Good Samaritans and have tried to reciprocate as much as we can. That's what neighbors should do. You help each other out and you become friends.

Chapter 84

The Wisdom of C.F. Butler

Ever since I can remember, I've been a clipper and a saver. When you want to remember something that catches your eye, it's the best way to "remember."

My mother was the same way. You might not keep it in your mind all those years, but you'll run across it from time to time and that triggers the memory.

I never met C.F. "Fred" Butler, the second-generation owner of the Exchange State Bank in Springville, because he died in 1941. But his father, Joseph S. Butler, founded the bank in 1878 and it was in the family until I bought it almost a century later.

Mr. Butler was a true community giver, donating to many worthwhile causes. During his life, he often wrote for the local newspaper and his words of wisdom later re-appeared in the paper. That's how clippings ended up in my files and why they're still there today.

In one clipping, "My Prayer for Today," Mr. Butler talks about honoring and respecting your parents, being honest in your dealings with other men, working hard to save a little and to give a little to others and to stay far away from feelings of jealousy, hatred and discontent.

Mr. Butler's words are timeless. They remind me of things my mother said.

That's why this item in particular needs to appear here:

Philosophy of Life

Did it ever occur to you that a man's life is full of crosses and temptations? He comes into the world without his consent, and goes out against his will, and the trip between is exceedingly rocky. The rule of contraries is one of the features of this trip.

When he is little, the big girls kiss him; when he is big, the little girls kiss him. If he is poor, he is a bad manager; if he is rich, he is dishonest. If he needs credit, he can't get it; if he is prosperous, everybody wants to do him a favor.

If he is in politics, it is for graft; if he is out of politics, he is no good to his country. If he doesn't give to charity he is a stingy cuss; if he does, it is for show. If he is actively religious, he is a hypocrite; if he takes no interest in religion, he is a hardened sinner.

If he gives affection, he is a soft specimen; if he cares for none, he is cold blooded. If he dies young, there is a great future for him; if he arrives at an old age, he missed his calling.

My mother used to tell me when a boy, tell the truth, work, and shun the devil, and I will add to this, mind your own damn business.

C.F. Butler

Chapter 85

New Shoes

Even though it has been a long, long time since I've worn shoes with holes in them, I occasionally still think of the days my mother put cardboard in my old ones to make them last longer. Especially when I shop for new shoes.

I bought some new shoes the other day. Rockport slip-ons. The funny part is, we were at the Tanger Outlet Mall near Williamsburg and I just wanted to buy one pair. But it was a lot cheaper buying two pair than just one pair, so I got a black pair and a brown pair. I always like to find a bargain.

The thing is, when you grow up that way, you don't change. You just keep on doing what you always did. I think I paid $59 for my glasses. They're bifocals. I wasn't going to pay $200. I got them at Payless Optical.

People interpret that type of thinking two ways. Some call it being cheap. Some call it being frugal. Either way, it doesn't bother me in the least. I just keep on doing it.

My sport coat is too big for me now since I've lost 35 pounds. I need to get a new one. I'll probably go to J.C. Penney. I buy most of my clothes there. I think we've got some coupons.

Sure Joanne and I clip coupons. As an example, yesterday, we used a coupon to buy a gallon of milk for

$1.99. We put the coupons in a drawer in the kitchen and use them when we go shopping. I use the fuel-saver card at Hy-Vee, too. You save money on gas with that.

Everybody watches the price of gas. It doesn't matter how much money you've got, you look at the gas prices when you see them on the signs. People get all upset about a nickel or a dime increase in a gallon of gas. They could pay closer attention to other expenses, too.

My friend Russ Gerdin, who started the successful Heartland Express trucking company, told me he never bought a new car for himself. One time I thought he got a new car but it was just another used one.

Before you buy anything, you need to determine if you need it. Or if it's something you just want. I think that's where people get into trouble with their credit cards.

I think credit cards are good. But, you have to be careful not to use them for too many somethings you don't need. If you can't pay it off every month, you shouldn't have a credit card.

When you grow up with a mother who watched the money like mine did, you learn to always wait for something to go on sale. When you're poor you don't have any choice.

That's why we actually did very little for Christmas and birthdays and other special occasions. When these anniversaries come along in your later years, you tend to do the same. They were never much of an added expense because we didn't make a big deal about them. They still aren't a big deal as a matter of habit.

If you grew up being frugal, you'll probably always be that way. There's nothing wrong with that.

Chapter 86

Looking Back

Reflections sometimes are interesting.

Looking back, I didn't think I had so much going for me but now I see that a lot of other people didn't have much, either. It was the 1930s when we grew up. The Great Depression.

Emma Buresh, Ernie's mother, works at her rug loom in her later years at the house Ernie built for his parents on the Shueyville farm.

You can see, as you're growing up in your teens and your twenties, there are so many things that affect your opinion of yourself. Of course, your parents have something to do with that. Despite my mother's encouragement, I always felt a little below everyone else. That turned out to not be a really bad thing. It energizes you to try to continually improve.

Ernie Buresh's father, Joe, milks a cow during his days as a farmer near Shueyville.

Opportunities. There were so many I didn't recognize at the time and some I couldn't do anything about. Fortunately, I was able to choose opportunities that turned out well.

The best one was meeting Joanne. Marrying Joanne. The Good Lord kind of took care of me.

Joanne and I seldom have major arguments. She's a strong-willed German. I'm a strong-willed Czech. Sometimes, the best thing to do is drop it. You just don't want to argue when it's not going to do either one of you any good. It can do more harm. Move on. There are so many other things you can talk about.

Joanne was a better student than I ever was. I was just average and Wendy says average isn't that bright. In my opinion, though, after Joanne and I got together we were better than average. Sometimes that's what it takes – another person to bring you up, to make you

279

better. I know Joanne would agree. We are good together.

Joanne's dad was great to us and helped us build a lot of confidence. But there was a time he wondered about me and that's when we bought the farm. It came up when we had a lot of obligations with the medical bills for Sandy. He was wondering if we should be spending money on the farm. It worked out.

Of course we miss Joanne's dad, but we also miss Howard and Margaret Hall a lot. You couldn't have asked for a better mentor than Howard when you're starting a career. Mine just happened to be banking. I know it's been more than 40 years that he's been gone but I sure miss him.

Moving to Anamosa was like going home for Joanne so it was kind of exciting. That tied us closer to her dad and to Howard who were both from Onslow. And how fortunate could you be to sell a house for the same price as the one you wanted to buy and to have the new house be so much better? If I didn't realize that luck was on my side before that, I certainly realized it then.

Looking back, though, the one blessing I had that made the rest of my life so enjoyable was my health. To be healthy for 88 years, to be able to have a hip replacement at 88 years old, is all amazing. A lot of factors play into that but there's one you can't discount. That is luck.

Chapter 87

A New Hip

The pain is gone. My physical therapist said it was time to get to work.

Let me tell you, I never thought I'd feel this good. My hip hurt for so long and it kept getting worse. Near the end, before I had surgery to replace it, I couldn't walk anywhere without using a cane. One day, walking downstairs to my office at Hilltop, the wooden cane snapped in two. It just broke and I fell several steps to the bottom. It scared me more than it hurt, but it made me realize how badly I needed my hip replaced. I couldn't live that way.

Before surgery I moved into a room at The Woodlands at Meth-Wick in Cedar Rapids. That's where I had to do my recovery after surgery, too. Occupational therapy in the morning, physical therapy in the afternoon until I could walk. I'd gone from the wooden cane to a metal one and then a walker with four wheels. I could move from one chair to the other with the cane but I was awfully unsteady.

The day of the surgery I got up at 4:30 in the morning. That was natural because I was always getting up early. With my hip I couldn't sleep in bed so I slept in my recliner. It was comfortable, but not for a whole night.

Out by 5:30 that morning, I arrived at University Hospitals and was prepped for surgery by 7:30. It would take two hours. They told me I'd be able to tell something was going on, but I don't remember anything. That's good.

They had me spend the first night in the ICU so they could prepare my room. It was easier that way and they could keep an eye on me. Surgery was a Wednesday. The next day I moved into my room and Monday I was back at Meth-Wick.

In the ICU they had me stand up while they changed the sheets on the bed. It had only been a few hours. Amazing. I was on medication so it didn't hurt. I can't tell one pain from another, anyway. But I tell you one thing, painkillers make you goofy.

I had the weirdest dream. I was stuck in a place and I didn't know where it was or how to get out of it. Ron Corbett, the mayor of Cedar Rapids and a good friend, sent the fire department out. They rescued me on a stretcher. The story made the front page of The Gazette. I absolutely didn't know where I was and then, suddenly, I woke up. Do you know how frightening that is?

Sunday morning at 7:30 I was sound asleep when somebody tapped me on the shoulder. He said, "Come on Ernie, let's go for a walk." I didn't understand.

It was John Callaghan, the orthopedic surgeon who replaced my hip. He had a wheelchair. He put me in the wheelchair and said "Let's take a tour of the hospital."

He wheeled me around and we went up to the eighth floor and out on the veranda. It was cold. He said, "Fresh air will do you good." It was so cold.

But here's this surgeon, so talented he designed the new hip I've got, and he takes the time to wheel me around. Wow.

So many people sent me flowers and came up to see me. Dr. Carter and his wife sat with me and watched the Iowa women's basketball team play in the NCAA

Tournament. Dr. Ghosh stopped in and brought me tulips. Lynette Marshall from the University of Iowa Foundation visited. Ken Kates, who is in charge of the hospital, visited me several times.

When a person gets into his 80s and you have a weird dream and people do things for you, it's a new chapter in your life. I was in a phase where I had trouble controlling my emotions. I've never been externally emotional, but you have these people like Dr. Callaghan who are really committed to helping you. How can you be any other way?

The whole experience was incredible. All of the things that happened before, during and after my surgery are what this book is all about. All of the good things. The world is so full of good people.

I'm 88. Can anybody have been any luckier?

When something like this happens, you can see that you need to go through life and enjoy your friends, your accomplishments, the positive things that happen to you, more than you ever realized before.

Chapter 88

Coming Home:

Looking Forward to 89

There's no place like home. That's what Sandy always said after we'd been on vacation.

Having my hip replaced was no vacation. But I was gone from Hilltop for five weeks. I really missed it. There's nothing like being home.

We've lived at Hilltop for more than 25 years. We're the second owners. It's a two-story brick house designed by Paul Williams, a famous architect from Los Angeles, Calif., that was built in the 1930s for Weaver Witwer who owned the Me Too grocery stores and several farms. He gave it the name Hilltop because it's on a hill off East Post Road that overlooks southeast Cedar Rapids. The hill is high enough so our view is above the treetops.

Even though there are other houses around Hilltop, when Joanne and I sit in the hearth room and look out the windows we feel like we're up here alone. It's a cozy area that makes you appreciate being alive. We're visited by deer and turkeys all the time. Right now it's my favorite place to be.

In 2004, a write-up about our house was in The Gazette. Shirley Ruedy really captured it well. We've saved the clipping – like I save everything. In that story she quoted me – "I was born and raised on a farm near Shueyville. I was born poor, and I never forget my heritage. I've been lucky."

Hilltop, the home of Joanne and Ernie Buresh for more than 25 years, overlooks southeast Cedar Rapids.

That sums it up.

Since growing up poor, I've learned that life is a series of transitions. Remember when you didn't have to lock your doors? Now we have alarms and video surveillance and lock the doors if we go up the street. That's a shame.

Joanne and I have been trying to downsize for years, but when it comes to that I have two problems – I'm Czech and I hate to throw anything away.

Before my hip surgery we thought it might be best to move into a condominium. That way we'd be forced to get rid of a lot of things. And I'd be able to get around better since Hilltop has a lot of stairs. But we decided to see how my recovery went first and we're both

285

amazed. Since I've started regular physical therapy my hip works better than it has in a long time. The pain is gone and I hope to get rid of my cane soon. I can walk around the house, except for the stairs, without it. I've been lucky.

When I was recovering at Meth-Wick, a young man delivered a recliner to my room so I'd have a comfortable place to sit. He guessed that I was 68 years old. I laughed. And I felt good about it. He was only twenty years off. I turn 89 on Oct. 28. I can't believe it.

As I look back on 88 years, I may have grown up poor but my whole life was full of opportunity. Opportunity is nothing unless you develop relationships to go with it. As I look back on my life, the best thing is all of the friends we have.

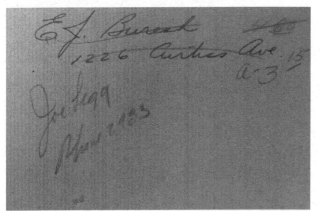 

Joe Legg of Anamosa, a neighbor of Ernie Buresh's in 1963, graduated from Iowa State a year after Ernie but used this textbook that had previously been used by Ernie. Joe returned the book to Ernie earlier this year.

In fact, here's an example. On a trip to Anamosa the other day we saw Esther and Joe Legg who were our neighbors for 29 years. Joe gave me this old book he purchased used at the book store when he attended Iowa State. He opened it up and there was my name. He'd scratched it out and written his name below it. I graduated from the engineering college in 1948 and he graduated from the college of agriculture in 1949. We never knew each other then. In 1963 when we moved to Anamosa we became friends. Now he gives me this book. Can you believe a book comes home 67 years later?

The Good Lord has really blessed us in so many ways. Health-wise. Friends-wise. We have enough money to pay our bills. I don't know what more you'd want in retirement than what we have, even though I still feel I'm not retired because Joanne and I stay so busy.

It seems like every time we turn around somebody's coming to visit us or we've got a function to attend at the Czech museum or St. Luke's Hospital, the University of Iowa, Cornell College . . . we can accept the invitations if we want to or we can stay home.

It's so wonderful to be able to drive again. I couldn't do that for almost two months while recovering. I'm supposed to get fitted for hearing aids. I can hear fine but they don't think I can. We'll see.

I really don't want to go anywhere – at least not far. I've seen what I want to see. Joanne and I get back to Anamosa frequently. We like to eat at the Ox Yoke in the Amana Colonies. We continue to visit the University of Iowa.

We've got the best friends anybody could have. There's no way you could make a list that's any better. That's what you need as you grow older. We took care of our wants a long time ago. We've got each other. We're at Hilltop. We're home.

A wooden sculpture created by Cedar Rapids artist Richard Pinney that hangs in Ernie Buresh's den sums up his life, from the names of his children to banking, playing bridge, building a house, the longstanding relationship with the University of Iowa Hawkeyes and even the idea that Ernie has never worn a watch yet always manages to be on time.

Index

Authors

Ernie Buresh, born a Czech protestant, left behind a poor childhood around Shueyville, Iowa, to serve in the Army, graduate from Iowa State with a degree in agricultural engineering and earn a law degree from the University of Iowa. He started his own feed business and then moved into banking, owning several Eastern Iowa banks in a career that spanned more than five decades. For years, many of his friends urged him to write a book. After coming up with a title, "The Advantage of Being Born Poor," in the 1990s, Ernie is pleased to have completed his book.

Dave Rasdal, a native Iowan, spent more than 35 years as a journalist in the state including 30 years as author of the "Ramblin'" feature column about people, places and things in The (Cedar Rapids) Gazette. He has published two books of his columns and is currently working on a variety of fiction and non-fiction book-length manuscripts.